By Hereditary Virtues:
a History of Lough Rynn

Fiona Slevin

Coolabawn Publishing

Coolabawn Publishing

By Hereditary Virtues: a History of Lough Rynn

First published in 2006
by Coolabawn Publishing

www.loughrynn.net.

A version published as a monograph in 1997.

ISBN no. 0 9553883 0 9
978 0 9553883 0 9

To my parents, Tim and Tina Slevin.

Acknowledgements

Many people helped with the production of this book. I give sincere thanks to all and to the following in particular: To both my parents for encouraging me to write it; To my mother who acted as agent, marketing manager, sales-person, inventory controller and PR agent during my first attempt to print this back in 1997; To my brother Michael who, with his encyclopaedic knowledge and attention to detail, corrected inaccuracies, provided images, maps and stories, and added facts that probably only he knows, and who was always at the end of the 'phone in the last few days and nights of frantic editing; To my friend Sadhbh who indulged me by reading an early draft from cover to cover and whose enthusiasm reignited my excitement in the venture (and who always preferred 'By Hereditary Virtues'); To my friend Natasha who gave me much-appreciated practical advice and confidence-boosting support; To Gráinne Murray who generously found time to meet my ridiculously short deadline to design the wonderful cover; To the people who bought my original version and offered me generous feedback, new stories and the motivation to do more; To all the people, shops and outlets who sold the original, thus inspiring me to do the whole thing a bit more properly; I particularly thank Paul Greenan of Paul's in Mohill, Nick Kaszuk and Joanna Moss of the excellent Trinity Rare Books in Carrick-on-Shannon, Meehan's in Mohill, Dunne's and the Tourist Office in Carrick-on-Shannon, the Libraries in Mohill and Ballinamore, Martina Fox at Lough Rynn House (who also provided practical encouragement to write this version), and my mother again for promoting the story so well to guests at Coolabawn House over their bacon and sausages; To the many people who read much of this story on my website and who took the time to email me and write complementary and informative notes in my guestbook; To Matt Gaffey, who taught me History at Marion College, Mohill, from whom I first learned that history is about people and who introduced me to Francisco de Cuellar; To the library staff at the Leitrim County Library in Ballinamore, the National Library of Ireland in Dublin, the British Library in London, the British Newspaper Library in London; To all those who live in the area who continue to make this a living history.

While all of the above individuals played their part in bringing this book to fruition and while facts and assertions are drawn from authoritative sources, all opinions are my own, and I take full responsibility for any errors, inaccuracies and omissions.

For further reading on the topic, please visit my website at www.loughrynn.net and Michael Slevin's at www.mohill.com. The former contains some text and data that did not fit into the book and will also contain updates to my research as I learn more. My brother started www.mohill.com as the home-page for my mother's long-standing Bed & Breakfast at Coolabawn House in Mohill but it quickly turned into the most comprehensive repository of information and stories about every facet of Mohill you can think of and more besides. Both sites have Guest-books: please use them to pass on comments, feedback and stories of your own, or feel free to email me at fiona.slevin@loughrynn.net.

Preface

This book has had a long gestation period. My interest in local history was sparked by a couple of things: one was spending many happy school breaks cycling out to Lough Rynn and being intrigued by the Castle and the gardens; the other was talking to Irish-American visitors to our house who wanted to learn about their roots.

Although I remember the Clements family still living at the Castle, for most of my childhood the house lay vacant and the grounds were overgrown. I often went out to Lough Rynn, sometimes on my own and sometimes with friends, and revelled in the lush walks and crumbling walls and the calm stillness of the lake. I always felt that the place was imbued with a sense of sadness and despair, as if still haunted by the ghosts of desperate tenants and their despotic landlord. It had the loudest silence of anywhere I knew. While I recognised an over-active imagination at work, I did want to know more about the reality of the lives of the people who had lived and worked there, if only to give my imaginings depth.

At the same time, we had a continuous flow of Americans staying at our home for Bed & Breakfast. Many were visiting relatives in the area and came year after year; others might be second or third-generation, in Ireland for the first time, and seeking to trace their ancestry. I frequently found myself in the role of unofficial genealogical and historical advisor. Over time, I thought it judicious to learn something about the history of the area rather than relying on hearsay and patchy data. It began to get embarrassing when visitors would ask me questions I couldn't answer, or worse, know more than I did. Given that my parents were blow-ins to Mohill, I wasn't going to be able to rely on family sources for information. Instead, I listened to local people who had many personal stories of the estate and especially of Lord Leitrim. Inspired by these, I was compelled to learn more.

I started my research informed by, it has to be said, a rather prejudicial view of Lord Leitrim. I was surprised to find that the reality was more challenging. Yes, he committed some deeds that warranted a reputation as a despotic oppressor of poor tenant farmers; but he also was a radical liberal who worked to improve the welfare of the land and the people and who was active during the Famine in relief efforts. Why did only his evil reputation survive? And why was he singled out for demonisation when the class tension that characterised the period was a much more complex issue?

I spent many a happy hour in the National Library in Dublin and found it wondrously amazing to be given the actual original rent books and letters and documents from the estate: as I gingerly unfolded a letter or notebook that might not have been opened since it had been put away by the original addressee, I would feel a surge of excitement at being the one to discover it. For me, these personal accounts made the era and people come alive and gave more meaning to events that were happening at national level.

While Lord Leitrim's era takes up most of the pages of this book, I start as far back as the original settlement of the area by the MacRaghnaill clann. The MacRaghnaill's chieftaincy, and the Irish clann way of life, disappeared in the 1600s, but its influences on today's geography, society and culture have not. For instance, the boundary of the current county of Leitrim reflects a boundary that was established back in the 600s; the names Reynolds, Mulvey and Darcy remain common in the area; and even today there is a discernible difference in accent between Mohill and Carrigallen that remarkably reflects an old clann border that should have disappeared four hundred years ago.

If you progress further than this page and read even a few of the following chapters, you will find that facts and figures and laws are only interesting to me as context for understanding people—both powerful and powerless—as they lived out their lives, day by day. Who were they? What did they eat? How did they live? What drove them? And, as importantly, how did these people shape the people and society we are today. We may all have more inherited virtues, attributes and characteristics than we might sometimes think.

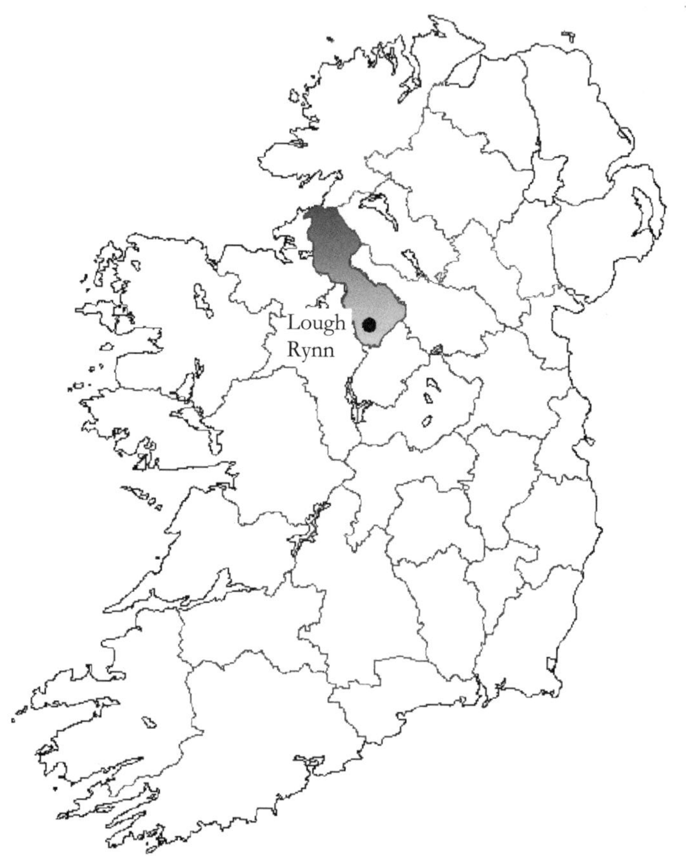

Fig. 1: Map of Ireland with Lough Rynn marked

Contents

Figures and illustrations

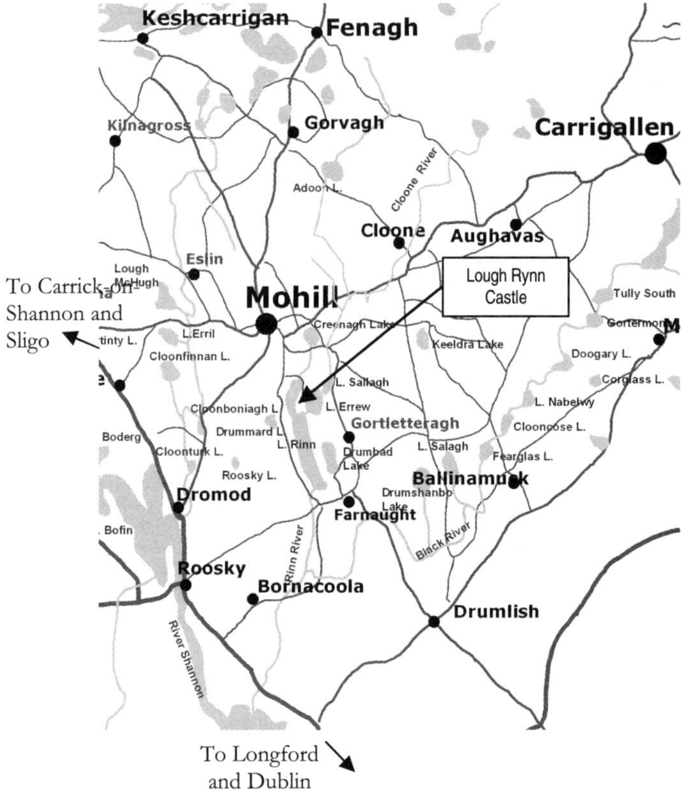

Fig. 2: Lough Rynn and Mohill Co. Leitrim, Ireland

Introduction

The mention of the name Lord Leitrim can still evoke strong feelings and memories in the people of Co. Leitrim. Although nearly 130 years have passed since the local Landlord was assassinated, the impact of his time and tenure on the people of the area has only in recent years begun to dissipate.

As in much of Ireland, South Leitrim suffered greatly during the 1800s. Famine, disease and emigration were a constant in the lives of many for much of the first half of the century and of course hit a terrible peak mid-century with the Great Famine. After the Famine, the emigration continued and a new era of political unrest and social change gained increasing pace. It was in this context that Lord Leitrim, William Sydney Clements, 3rd Earl of Leitrim, dominated the lives of thousands of people in ways that was in turn beneficent and destructive. By the end of his life, he was seen as one of the most disreputable landlords of 19th century Ireland and owned estates that stretched from Kildare in the east to Galway in the west and right up to Donegal in the far North of Ireland. He ran this huge landholding from his base at Lough Rynn Castle, near Mohill in the southern end of County Leitrim.

The manor house at Lough Rynn has always been referred to as Lough Rynn Castle. It was built in an idyllic position on the shores of the lake from which it takes its name. It lies at the end of a long, tree-lined drive, some five kilometres from the town of Mohill. The Castle still stands (now transformed into a luxury hotel) and it, along with the outhouses and extensive gardens, present a tangible legacy from Lord Leitrim's time. Less visible, but arguably more potent, was the Earl's influence on the lives of the people in the area. In the mid-19th century, he was responsible for thousands of people who lived on and off his estates and exercised immense control over the local economy and social structures. The Earl's persona makes an interesting study on its own, but given that his era coincided with a period of enormous social, economic and political change in Ireland, a review of his life and times yields fascinating insights into the lives of all the people who lived and worked during this time.

In many ways the history of Lough Rynn represents a microcosm of the history of the country, but in other ways it is an exception. Unusually, the first major settlement (by the MacRaghnaill clann[1]) would last nearly a thousand years, until the 1600s. Leitrim largely escaped the Viking raids between

---

[1] Long before the MacRaghnaills, some 3,500 years ago, Bronze Age dwellers used high ground a short way from the Castle as a burial place. The site named Druids Hill is still marked by the dolmen they built there.

874 and 950 and was one of a handful of counties that escaped the 12th century Norman invasion. Subsequently, however, it was one of the first to be settled by the English in the 1600s. This meant that the old Irish feudal system and traditions continued in Leitrim far longer than in other counties but then disappeared much quicker with the arrival of English settlers. The significant social, economic and political shifts that took place during the mid-nineteenth century thus had their roots in the changing patterns of land ownership and society in the centuries and decades before.

Through the 18th and 19th centuries, under descendants of the English settlers, Lough Rynn experienced greater levels of benevolence and reform but also of autocracy and tyranny than in many other areas. The Clements family who owned Lough Rynn for 250 years were noteworthy and distinct from many of their ascendancy peers in terms of their financial acumen, artistic interests and talents, politically activism, liberal and radical views and strongly held sense of duty. And unlike most of their peers, they considered themselves Irish.

For many reasons, the history of Lough Rynn in the 19th century is of most interest to us. The consequences and impact of events and people of this time still live with us and it is close enough in time to touch us personally: our great-great grandparents could have lived on the Lough Rynn Estate during Lord Leitrim's time. Certainly the names listed in the census and rent books of the time remain common in the area: names like Reynolds, Moran, Shanley and Conefrey.

In studying the history of Lough Rynn, we are fortunate that a collection of unique manuscript and archive materials from

Lough Rynn has survived. Early Annals provide an overview of events that shaped people's lives in the middle part of the millennium; records like Lord Leitrim's personal account book, contemporary local newspapers, the estate account books and rent ledgers, as well as state and local papers, provide a unique and superlative record of day-to-day life in the 19th century.

While the main part of this book recounts the life and times of the 3rd Earl of Leitrim, it also attempts to place his life in a wider context. It traces the lives of those who came before and after him and sets all of these against a background of major national and local events.

In writing any passages involving the 3rd Earl of Leitrim, I use a range of titles and names. William Sydney Clements was known to his family as Sydney, therefore I refer to him thus during his younger days. On the death of his brother, he attained the title Viscount, Lord Clements. Any reference to Viscount Clements or Lord Clements or Clements refers to William Sydney Clements during the years 1839 to 1854. To avoid confusion, I do not use these titles in referring to his brother, Robert (who held the titles before him). In 1854, Sydney became 3rd Earl of Leitrim, Lord Leitrim; references to him after that time use these titles. Similarly, to avoid confusion, I avoid using the title 'Lord Leitrim' to refer to any other Earls of Leitrim.

Fig. 3: Lough Rynn Castle from the back

Fig. 4: Lough Rynn Castle from the front

Lough Rynn before the 1600s

For a thousand years, Lough Rynn was home to the MacRaghnaill (Reynolds) clann. The first MacRagnaills to settle there were a branch of the Conmaicne people who arrived from the present Dunmore in County Galway[2] in the first quarter of the sixth century. The Conmaicne settled first in Magh Réin (Fenagh), and gradually spread through all of south Leitrim. The settlers became known as the Conmaicne Réin and comprised a number of clanns including 'Muintir Eolais' (MacRagnaills), Muintir Cearbhallain (O'Mulvey), and Cinel Luachain (MacDarcy). Each quickly moved to establish a distinct territory, and soon Muintir Eolais/MacRagnaills held sway in an area that covered "all the level portion of County Leitrim south of Sliabh an Iarainn", including the area around Mohill and Lough Rynn.

---

[2] Another branch of the Conmaicne headed west – these were known as the "Conmaicne Mara" and of course gave their name to a place we know as Connemara in West Co. Galway.

Fig. 5: The remains of the MacRagnaill castle at Lough Rynn

The MacRaghnaills made Lough Rinn[3] their main seat[4] and sometime in the 12th century, built a stone castle by the shores of the lake, the ruins of which still stand. The structure is fairly standard for the time, but it did have a few unusual and clever features. Although a square shape, the castle had rounded corners that made it more impervious to artillery attacks and it had a straight stairway carved into the hollow of a wall, rather than the more usual spiral stair in one corner. The castle lasted nearly three hundred years until

[3] Lough Rynn generally refers to the estate. The lake and the river linking it to the Shannon are generally spelled Lough Rinn (or Rinn Lake) and the Rinn River respectively.

[4] In later years (1570), the principal castle was on an island on Lough Scur.

1474 when it was destroyed in a 'great war' with a neighbouring clann. The castle site was well chosen. As well as providing some protection on one side, the lake offered further sanctuary in the form of an ancient crannóg, a round, thatched hut built on stilts a little way out from the shoreline. It had been built hundreds of years previously, but was almost certainly used by the MacRaghnaills up to the 16th century.

Like other clanns in the area, the MacRaghnaills devoted much of their time to defending and holding on to their land and their cattle. The Annals of the Four Masters makes several references to the exploits of the MacRaghnaills, recording many incursions and battles between them and their neighbours. In 1253, the entire country of Muintir Eolais was plundered by a coalition of O'Reillys, O'Connors, and O'Farrells. Battles ensued, centred around Carrigallen, Cloone and Annaduff. Eventually, MacRaghnaill regained his castle and defeated O'Reilly in a "fierce battle where many were slain".

In 1367 MacRaghnaill, O'Connor and MacTiernan, accompanied by a troop of gallowglasses[5], attempted to take Moylurg in Roscommon but returned "without having gained booty or consideration". MacRaghnaill's later defeat is recorded with some regret, for he was "a good, rich and affluent man".

---

[5] Mercenary soldiers, mostly from Scotland

When the battles were nearer home and when Lough Rynn proved unsafe, the MacRaghnaills had friends at the nearby monastery in Mohill[6]. On occasion, they sought refuge there as they retreated from battle or escaped from siege.

In 1345, Lough Rynn was the scene of a major battle during which Turlough O'Connor, King of Connaught met his death. Turlough had come to Rynn to assist Tadhg MacRaghnaill against the Clann Murtough but was shot by an arrow as he retreated west towards Annaduff. The Annals of the Four Masters record the deed:

> Turlough, son of Hugh, son of Owen O'Connor, King of Connaught was killed in Autumn by one shot of an arrow at Fidh Doradha[7] in Muintir Eolais after he had gone to Loch Airinn to aid Teigh MacRaghnaill against the descendants of Muirchertach Muimhneach O'Connor. The Clann Murtough and some of the Muintir Eolais pursued him as far as Fidh Doradha and killed him at Gurtin na Spideoiga. For a long time before, there had not fallen of the Gaels any one more lamented than he. Hugh, son of Turlough was inaugurated King in his place.

---

[6] The Franciscans had established the monastery in the 12th century, though it had been a monastic settlement since the 500s. According to the Annals of Tighernach, St. Manchan of Mohill died in 538AD (*Manchan Maethla cecídit*)

[7] Fedora, near Annaduff, Mohill

At the time of his death, Turlough had reigned for 21 years. According to the Annals of Clonmacnoise, "there was not a greater exploit done by an arrow" since the killing 900 years earlier of the great High King of Ireland, Niall of the Nine Hostages. (It was the major event in an otherwise bountiful year: the Loch Cé Annals notes that "this was the best year that had ever come for nuts, and the produce of the earth, and of cattle, and of trees and herbs".) Many of the remaining accounts record a litany of feuds and wars mingled with treachery and pestilence. After which they may well have consoled themselves with a drop of whiskey, though the perils of over-imbibing were clear. The oldest reference to whiskey in Ireland, written in 1405, relates how the 'water of life' became the 'water of death' for a potential chieftain, Richard MacRaghnaill:

> "Risderd Mag Ragnaill, eligible for the chieftainship of the Muinter Eolais, entered into rest after drinking 'water of life' to excess; it was deathly water to him"

Following decades of continuous feuding, Lough Rynn castle was finally destroyed in 1474 during "a great war between Mag Ragnaill and the posterity of Maelsechlainn Mag Ragnaill". Thereafter, the MacRaghnaills appear to have lost their independence. They were forced to submit to O'Rourke in 1526, when O Ruairc "made a great hosting into Muinter Eolais, obtaining power over every region of the land and at last forcing them against their will to yield him pledges and hostages".

From the mid-1500s, the clann way of life was under serious threat. An increasingly powerful English administration was slowly but surely extending its influence and dominion. In a visit to Mohill in 1540, the 'Saxons' destroyed the monastery and beheaded the guardian and several of the friars. By 1590, the English government forces were actively routing the local clanns. In March that year, "an immense army" fought against the forces of O'Rourke and MacRaghnaill. After spending the night in Mohill they made away with 1,000 cattle–a major blow to the wealth and health of the clann. This practice by the English of swooping down on villages to take their cattle was a common one and is described in one of the best accounts of the time written by a Captain of the Spanish Armada, Francisco de Cuellar. De Cuellar had been shipwrecked off the Sligo coast and was given shelter by O'Rourke in north Leitrim. He describes the living conditions of the people:

> "They live in huts made of straw. The men have big bodies . . . and are as agile as the deer. They eat but one meal a day, and that at night, and their ordinary food is bread of an oaten kind and butter. They drink sour milk . . . but no water, although it is the best in the world. On feast-days they eat meat, half-cooked, without bread or salt. They dress in tight breeches and goatskin jackets cut short but very big. Over all they wear a blanket or cloak and they wear their hair down to their eyes. Most of the women are pretty but ill-dressed. They wear nothing but a shift and a cloak

> over it and a linen cloth, much-folded on their heads and tied in front.

De Cuellar also remarks on the Irish propensity for continuous war with the English and with each other:

> "Their great bent is to be robbers and to steal from one another, so that not a day passes without a call to arms among them. For when the men of one village learn that there are cattle or anything else in another village, they go at once armed at night and shouting war-cries to kill one another."

The line of independent chieftains terminated with Brian O'Rourke, lord of Breffni and Minterolis. He renounced his allegiance to Elizabeth I and allied himself with Pope SixtusV and the King of Spain. However, he ended up having to flee to Scotland, where he was taken prisoner, brought to London and executed as a traitor. His last request was to be hanged in the Irish fashion, by a rope made of twisted willow.

In 1565, the MacRagnaill and O'Rourke lands were formed into a county named Leitrim by Sir Henry Sidney, the new 'baronies' following the original clann borders. Today's borders were refined in 1583.

Their lands confiscated, the Chieftainship of the MacRaghnaills and their way of life died forever when, in 1620, the English government engaged in a systematic clearance of Irish lands and the replacement of the indigenous Irish with loyal English settlers.

This 'Plantation' heralded a new era of social and political change that continues to reverberate today.

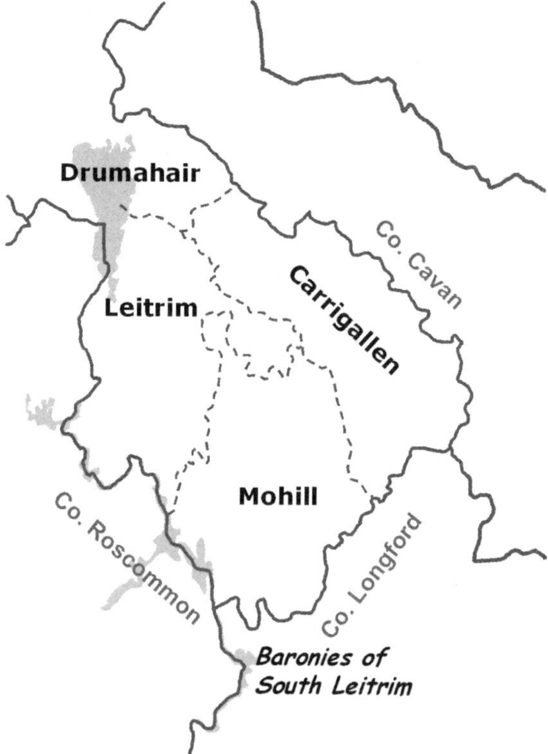

Fig. 6: Baronies of South Leitrim

The Plantation of Leitrim

Leitrim was one of the first counties to be handed over to English settlers in the Plantation of 1621 when the lands around Lough Rynn and the town of Mohill were given to the Crofton family. In the years following the Plantation, the Croftons brought over tenants from England to farm the land and the native Irish were gradually pushed out.

Any resistance from the Irish was forcefully repressed: in 1673, there was enough disturbance in Leitrim and elsewhere for Essex, the Lord Lieutenant General, to take action. In a decree in November that year, he forbade "persons of popish Religion" to "Ride with, carry, buy, use or keep in His or their House or Houses or elsewhere, any Muskets, Caliberts, Pistols, or other Guns whatsoever". Only two men in Leitrim were licensed to carry arms: Sir William Gore and Henry Crofton of Mohill.

By the late 1600s, by whatever means it had been achieved, William Molyneaux noted that Leitrim was "well planted with protestants" and that the native Irish were "civil, hospitable and ingenious". He also remarked that they were "very fond of their ancient chronicles and pedigrees": they abhorred theft and displayed a great love of music and fondness for news. He regretted, however, the way the Irish clung obstinately to their religion in "all its gaiety and superstitious forms".

The Penal Laws, implemented at the turn of the seventeenth century were the final nail in the coffin for native Irish landowners. These laws reinforced the already insidious social change by taking all normal rights away from Catholics. The 'Papists' were, for example, forbidden to own land; they had no inheritance rights, and they were forbidden to hold arms or to vote. They were also banned from the professions and public office. Effectively, the Laws aimed to clear the land of native Irish and reduce them to serfdom.

The Clements family

The Clements family's association with Lough Rynn began in 1749, when Nathaniel Clements bought about 10,000 acres in the Mohill area from Francis Seymour Conway, Lord Conway, 1st Marquess of Hertford and at the time, the Viceroy or Lord Lieutenant of Ireland.[8]

The Clements family had lived in Cavan since the mid-1600s when Daniel Clements, a junior ranking officer in Cromwell's army, was granted lands near Cootehill during the Plantation[9]. The lands had been confiscated from the ruling O'Reilly

[8] He was also "Lord of the Bedchamber" to King George III.

[9] Daniel's father, Richard was a substantial Leicestershire yeoman who emigrated with his family to America in 1642 and was amongst the first wave of English emigrants to settle in New England. One of Daniel's brothers remained there and became a Deputy to Massachusetts General Court and trial judge. Daniel, however, returned to England and then moved to Ireland to serve in Cromwell's army at bases in Belfast and Drogheda. By 1657, Daniel Clements was paying tithes on more than 1,000 acres at Rathkenny. The lands were confirmed under the Act of Settlement in 1667.

Clann, and were given to Clements in lieu of back-pay. Daniel went on to become High Sheriff of Cavan in 1674 and Justice of the Peace in 1675.

When James II, the Catholic King of England, arrived in Ireland, Daniel's son Robert was accused of treason and stripped of his lands. He fled back to England but was given back his lands after the accession of William III. He returned to Ireland as early as 1691, just a year after William defeated James at the Battle of the Boyne. On regaining his land, Robert immediately re-established himself in political and economic society. He held the positions of High Sheriff of Cavan and in 1711 was one of the original trustees of the Linen Manufacturers of Ireland. He was Member of Parliament for Newry between 1715 and 1722. He was also Teller of the Irish Exchequer. This latter position helped him to establish close links with the government and society leaders of the day. As significantly, it enabled him to demonstrate a strong financial acumen that he would pass down to his descendants.

Clements was clearly known to Jonathan Swift, author and Dean of St. Patrick's Cathedral in Dublin. In 1712, Swift wrote that Lord Anglesea, the Vice-Treasurer, thanked Swift for recommending Clements to him, saying he was "twenty thousand pounds the better for knowing Clements". No wonder Robert Clements was, according to Swift "mightily in Lord Anglesea's favour". Robert married well: his wife, Elizabeth Sandford of Maynooth extended the couple's holdings to include the Killadoon estates in County Kildare, where the Clements family eventually settled.

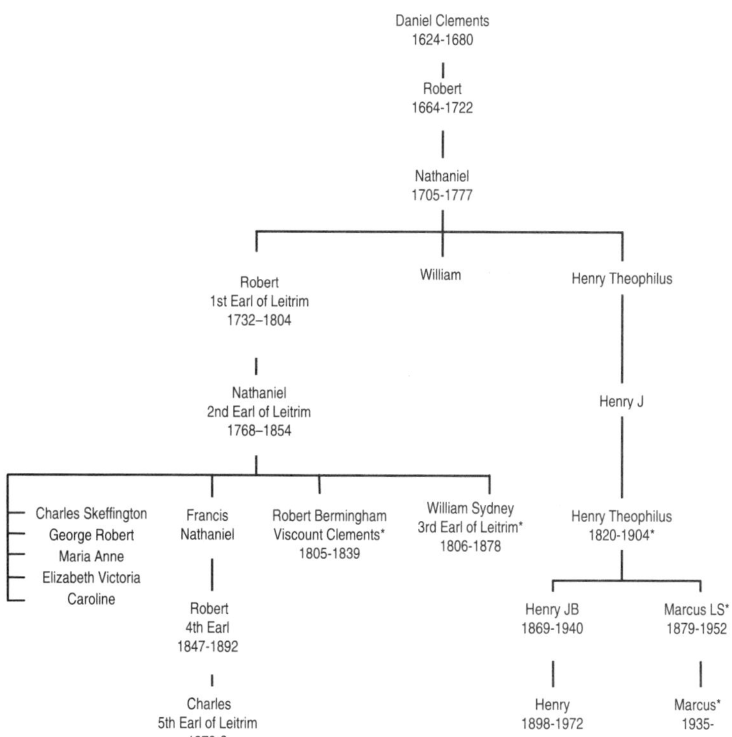

Fig. 7: Clements Family Tree

Nathaniel Clements 1705-1777

It was Robert's son Nathaniel Clements who, in 1749, purchased the lands around Lough Rynn. Nathaniel was an archetypal eighteenth century Ascendancy man and set out early to establish himself at the heart of Irish political, social and economic life. At 22, he became a Member of Parliament for Duleek—a seat he held until his death 51 years later. When Nathaniel acquired the Lough Rynn estate, the land was completely let to English and Irish tenants and he used the estate purely for extra income: he never lived there and his political roles and interests kept him occupied in Dublin and London. Three generations would pass before the estates became a primary residence for the Clements family.

Nathaniel Clements lived much of the time in Dublin, and enjoyed living in one of the most dynamic, progressive and sociable cities in Europe. This was Georgian Dublin: a period when the arts and commerce thrived and when some of the most beautiful buildings, streets and squares of Dublin were built. For those who had the means to fund it, life could be very good, with Dublin being viewed with envy (or disapproval) by visitors for its very active and profligate social life.

Nathaniel's absenteeism was not uncommon among Irish landlords. Lough Rynn, however, may have missed out more than most: Nathaniel was a distinguished amateur architect who had a great interest in the extensive building going on around Dublin. He shared this interest with his close friend and patron, the powerful and influential Luke Gardiner. Gardiner was Deputy Vice-Treasurer and Deputy Paymaster-General of Ireland. It says something of their relationship that Clements succeeded to both titles on Gardiner's retirement in 1755. Gardiner introduced Clements to the architecture and business of developing the north side of Dublin.

Nathaniel himself is credited with developing the style of 'agricultural layout' where a main dwelling house was linked by quadrant walls to pavilions that housed stables, barns and byres. Through the 1750s, Nathaniel used the style in designing houses such as Colganstown and Newberry Hall. He can take credit for many of Dublin's Georgian houses, including the current Italian embassy and his own townhouses in Stephen Street and Henrietta Street. He also owned at least seven buildings in Sackville Street (now O'Connell Street) in Dublin.

In April 1751, Nathaniel was appointed Chief Ranger and Master of the Game in the Phoenix Park, which included Chapelizod House, then the official residence of the Viceroys of Ireland. The house he designed as his own home was to reflect the grandeur and importance of his titles and his position in Dublin society. The house was sited in the Phoenix Park and completed in 1754. (In 1782, the house was sold to the government by Nathaniel's son, Robert, for £25,000. It was added to and developed into the official residence for the Viceroys of Ireland; in the 20th century, it became Áras an Uachtaráin, the official residence of the Irish President.)

Nathaniel followed his father into the position of Teller of the Exchequer in 1728 and held the position for twenty-seven years. It was in this role that he showed himself to be an accomplished all-rounder, both artist and financier.

While his father had been known for making others rich, Nathaniel used the position to increase his own wealth. As Teller, he was responsible for disbursing money to officers, pensioners and members of the military establishment. He seized the opportunity to develop this role into a private banking service. Instead of paying out money, he offered to hold payments in private accounts for officers. In some cases he offered a loan or overdraft on which he received interest. This was no small facility: in 1746-'47 he earned £760 as agent to forty-two individuals and received £764.14.11 in interest on advances to thirteen of them. In the following year, his banking profits rose to £2,594—more than many of the Dublin Banks reported for the same period.

When he became Deputy Vice-Treasurer in 1755, Nathaniel no longer had the use of Treasury cash, but his accumulated gains were enough to enable him to set up a bank with two partners, Anthony Malone and Arthur Gore. Nathaniel funded his share out of his current bank account of £92,405.

The bank was set up in 1758 and paid interest on deposits of 2.33%—something quite unknown at the time. By January 1759, Nathaniel's bank account was showing a credit balance of the enormous sum of £155,330. His banking partnership however, only lasted a year and an Act of Parliament put a stop to any further banking activity by holders of public funds. (Nathaniel's son, Henry Theophilus, came close to emulating his father's banking career a generation later when, as an army agent, he handled large sums of public funds.) Despite the closure of his bank, Nathaniel Clements became one of the most powerful members of the House of Commons and was raised to the Privy Council.

In his private life, Nathaniel was also successful. He and his wife, Hannah, were popular amongst the social set in Dublin and London and were admired by the influential social commentators. In 1759, Mrs. Delaney, an influential society matron, commented gushingly on the couple's style, wealth and general deportment.

> "Not hear of Mrs Clements! Why she is finer than the first lady in England. Dresses, furniture, house, equipage—excelling all. . . .They set out in life very young and very humble, though both of good families. He . . . has gathered together by degrees an immense fortune if one may judge by the magnificence of his living; and what is quite surprising, they are both very moderate in understanding and yet there is a cleverness and elegance in everything about them that is beyond what could have been expected".

No doubt the Clements had been guests at one of Mrs. Delaney's routs where they would have feasted lavishly and played cards and danced the night away.

Having achieved so much in all aspects of his life, Nathaniel was thwarted in only one ambition: he wanted a title and an earldom for the family. One might have thought that, with all he had going for him, he would be successful. But despite persistent efforts to elevate the family, he died unrewarded.

Rynn in the 1700s

Little is known about Lough Rynn specifically during this period, but there is no reason to believe that life here was any different to other parts of the country.

Unlike Nathaniel Clements, most of the landed classes' income came through rents from their estates. And in contrast to the landlords' affluent, opulent lives, their tenants were living lives of poverty and starvation and were barely able to generate enough income to pay their rents.

In the mid-1700s, while Dublin and other towns were thriving, estates throughout the country were suffering frequent famines. While not on the scale of the Great Famine a hundred years later, they were bad enough to cause horrific crises. Contemporary travellers through the country remarked consistently on the misery and poverty of the people and the land. In 1732, Jonathan Swift noted that while the land was ill-used and not "turned to half its advantage", it was in better shape than the people. The "faces and habits and dwellings" of the natives were so terrible that one would "hardly think himself in a land where law, religion or common humanity is professed". As ever there was a big difference in the lives of the rich and the poor: it was through this same land that Turlough O'Carolan the famous harpist and composer (and a friend of Swift's) travelled with his harp, entertaining at the big houses across Ireland. O'Carolan's home base was a farm at Lakefield near Mohill. His wife, Mary, and his seven children lived there while O'Carolan lived out his role as the 'last of the Irish Bards': he travelled the roads of Ireland, staying with wealthy patrons along the way where he received food and lodging in exchange for entertaining the house, or maybe for composing a tune or 'planxty'.[10] O'Carolan died in 1738, marking an end not only to the bardic tradition in Ireland, but also to a whole way of life.

The mid-1700s was a period of huge change in Ireland. The country's population doubled in the eighteenth century to nearly five million; by 1841 it had increased to over eight million, with the period between 1780 and 1830 experiencing the most rapid growth.

Although it is unclear why this increase occurred, and at such a rate, there are a few notable contributory factors. One significant factor was the arrival of the potato which had been famously introduced by Sir Walter Raleigh in the early 1600s.

---

[10] O'Carolan is credited with coining the term 'planxty' to describe the songs he wrote in tribute to one of his hosts or to commemorate a marriage or funeral.

Fig. 8: Turlough O'Carolan

By the 1780s, the potato formed the staple diet of the people. It had several advantages: it could be grown pretty much anywhere and even the smallest plot of land would yield a viable harvest.

Being so prolific and easily stored, it could provide food for nine months of the year. One acre of potatoes could support a family of six, even though each consumed an average of ten to fourteen pounds per day with little variety in their preparation: they were usually boiled over the open fire. The skins were usually given to the family's pig. And the potato diet led to improved health. It was nutritious: the only real nutrient it lacked was Vitamin A, making it a complete and cheap food. The only supplement needed for a balanced diet was butter-milk and bacon and the occasional fish and vegetables. The potato therefore can be credited for ending, for the most part, the famines of previous decades. Unfortunately, the lumper (the variety of potato most favoured by the poor and labouring classes) was highly susceptive to the fungus, 'phytophthora infestans'. The fungus, commonly known as blight, had spread from North America to Europe and caused severe hardship when it hit a potato crop. It would have devastating consequences in the mid-nineteenth century when successive seasons of blight destroyed the potato crop and caused widespread famine, disease and death.

In the early 1800s, life expectancy for Irish males was 38. While not much by today's standards, it compared well with other contemporary societies, and Irish men were two inches taller than their counterparts in Britain. By the nineteenth century, the rural population had adopted another staple, tea, and Guinness, launched in 1759, became popular along with the traditional and highly acclaimed Irish Whiskey. Although the Penal Laws were still on the statute book, by the mid-1750s, Irish (Catholic) tenants were being granted short leases on small plots of land. And the availability of such small tenancies encouraged young men and women to feel confident enough to set up home on their own. Much of the increase in population is due to the large families these young couples started to have, and they tended to have more surviving children than their contemporaries in Britain.

As tenancies increased, so did discontent with the punitive taxes and tithes imposed by the government and the Church. So-called 'Secret Societies' began to form across the country to give collective expression to the tenants' grievances. There were increasingly vocal calls for independence from England and freedom of religious expression. The French Revolution in 1789 acted as a further fillip to the aggrieved. In 1791, the Societies and rebels were given coherence and direction under Theobald Wolfe Tone and his 'Society of the United Irishmen': their expressed goal was independence for Ireland and emancipation of the Catholic population.

The Rebellion of 1798

The United Irishmen gained in force throughout the 1790s with a series of uprisings by local 'Defenders' across Ireland. It was all to end in failure with the Rebellion of 1798, when the insurgents were defeated at Ballinamuck, just across the border from Leitrim.

In the lead-up to 1798, Leitrim—like many other counties—saw its share of disturbances. There were continuous skirmishes throughout the county and a couple of noteworthy battles in 1793 and at Drumcollop in 1795. The Irish leaders had called on the French for support, and in

August 1798, they welcomed the arrival of three French frigates carrying over a thousand veterans of Napoleon's army. The force, under the command of General Humbert, landed at Killala in Mayo and quickly captured the town. They were joined by over two thousand Irish recruits and proceeded on a long march through Connaught, taking the town of Ballina and winning a significant victory at Castlebar. From Castlebar, they moved eastward, believing that they would meet up with victorious Irish forces on the way. Unfortunately, Humbert's intelligence was out of date, and the United Irishmen had been defeated at Granard. The early gains in Mayo were to be the French reinforcements' greatest and only success.

As the rebels moved down through Sligo into Leitrim, they encountered continuous problems. They had to abandon their artillery in Dromahair and they were harassed all along the route by government troops. On 7th September, they made their way through Fenagh, where yet again they had to deal with an attack from an English patrol, this time led by Colonel Robert Crawford. By the time they arrived that evening at Cloone, the rebels numbered 844 French soldiers and 1,500 Irish insurgents. All were utterly exhausted. If they had been wearied by their journey so far, they were completely done in by having to haul themselves and their cannon up a steep, marshy, boggy road to the village[11]. When they finally arrived, Humbert declared a period of complete

[11] The legacy of 1798 lives on in Cloone: the steep climb up Graffy Hill to the village is still referred to as the French Road, and the place where the troops rested continues to be called Camp field.

rest and the rebels welcomed a feast prepared by the locals. Legend has it that they partook of six bullocks roasted over a makeshift grill made from the gates of the Protestant graveyard.

The insurgents rested up for the night while their leaders debated their next step. There was conflicting intelligence and advice: at least one of the French Generals, Sarrazin, wanted to march towards Granard (and adhere to the original plan to join the United Irishmen there) and wanted to leave at midnight to keep ahead of the English troops whom he knew to be not far behind. Humbert, however, dined at the home of the local land agent, William West and there met the local parish priest Fr. Charles Redehan and a Franciscan friar from Aughavas, Anthony Dunne. Dunne was a fluent French speaker and is reputed to have persuaded Humbert of the hopelessness of his enterprise: he had learned that Granard had been a failure and that a huge government army was closing in. Dunne was right about the government army. On the same evening that Humbert and his forces were at Cloone, the Commander in chief of the English troops, General Cornwallis, was making his way from Carrick-on-Shannon to Mohill. Cornwallis received word of the French-Irish force in Cloone and despatched an order to General George Lake, then at Keshcarrigan, to march through the night to Cloone. From Mohill, Cornwallis ordered his troops to move towards Ballinalee to intercept the rebels. Between them, the army of Cornwallis and Lake now numbered somewhere between 20,000 and 35,000 soldiers. Back at Cloone, Humbert was entreated to delay his march so that he could be joined by 10,000 United Irishmen who were on their way. Humbert waited until morning. Unfortunately, the promised 10,000 reinforcements turned out to be a few hundred men armed with pikes. (It is said that Fr. Redehan dissuaded the new arrivals from following Humbert, convincing them that it was a lost cause.) News of the English army had spread and there was a frenzied departure of those French and Irish who chose to march. The rebels' confidence and capacity to fight was dealt a major blow when the chains to pull their heavy cannon could not be found. But as they left Cloone on that beautiful, sunny September morning, they were given a rousing send-off by the locals. They were rested, fed, had adequate provisions for their journey and ropes had been found to replace the lost chains. However, further misfortune befell them at Keeldra when the poor road conditions again caused trouble: the new ropes broke under the strain of hauling the heavy guns and munitions and much of the artillery had to be left behind or pulled by hand. They had marched only five miles when, at Ballinamuck, Humbert's men met the English forces. They were vastly outnumbered and were routed in a short, bloody battle. By twelve noon, after only three hours of fighting, Humbert surrendered: some five hundred rebels lay dead; the government losses were reported to be fifteen. The French survivors were given an honourable surrender and were treated as prisoners of war; the Irish supporters were hunted down, imprisoned and many were summarily hanged.

Robert Clements, 1st Earl of Leitrim 1732-1804

Nathaniel Clements died in 1777 having led a hugely successful life, but without acquiring the title he craved. He had, however, laid effective groundwork for his son Robert.

Robert was more political than his father and set his sights on gaining an earldom. The records show that he expended considerable effort on petitioning for the title and eventually succeeded through a combination of skilled political manoeuvring, social positioning and sheer persistence.

In his mid-twenties, Robert took over the management of his father's new estates in Leitrim. Although he did not live on the Lough Rynn estate, he used it as a springboard to establish his political career and gain social advancement. For the next fifty years he accumulated title after title and position after position. At 33, he married Elizabeth Skeffington, eldest daughter of Clotworthy Skeffington, 1st Earl of Massereene, thus cementing his position amongst the political and social élite.

Fig. 9: Robert, 1st Earl of Leitrim

Clement, Percival Wood, 1937

In 1759 he was appointed High Sheriff of Leitrim, and gave his address as Lough Rynn, Mohill—the first official recording of the name.

As well as carving a political career, Robert took care to establish himself in other important areas. Over the years, he took on a succession of administrative roles in Dublin, all of which proffered opportunities to create connections and establish relationships with influencers in government and society[12]. But by the 1780s, after nearly 30 years of focused positioning and persistent petitioning for a peerage, Robert had little to show for his efforts. In 1783, he wrote that he had suffered ignominiously at the hands of successive government officials and believed himself to be "ill-used". With his track record of public service, Robert had been certain that he would be awarded a seat on the Privy Council, and he had had repeated assurances from the Lord Lieutenant, Lord Buckingham that his application would be recommended "very particularly". He failed in his application, despite the support of peers like Lord Worthington, who in 1783, wrote a plea on his behalf:

---

[12] Robert Clements – aka, Controller Great & Small Customs, Port of Dublin 1758–1804; Commissioner for the Revenue 1772–'73; Member of Parliament for Dunleck, Cavan and Leitrim 1761–1767; Member of Parliament for Co. Donegal 1765–'68 and 1776–'83; Member of Parliament for Carrick 1768–'76; High Sheriff Co. Leitrim 1759; Ranger of Phoenix Park 1777–'87; Governor Co. Leitrim 1777; Baron Leitrim of Manor Hamilton 19 April 1783; Searcher, Packer and Gauger, Port of Dublin 1787; Viscount Leitrim 20 December 1793; Earl of Leitrim 6 October 1795.

> "Mr Clements pleads the support uniformly given to His Majesty's Government by himself and all his connections—a support which he pledges himself in the fullest manner to continue.
>
> I must earnestly entreat your Lordship to obtain His Majesty's decision on the claims above-mentioned and communicate with the gentleman concerned before the dissolution of Parliament which admits no delay."

The plea fell on deaf ears and the Privy Council seat was given to a Mr Foster instead. However, Robert's disappointment was short-lived: in April, he finally made progress when he was made Baron Leitrim of Manor Hamilton.

But he was not satisfied: after all those years of faithful service to the government, Robert thought he deserved more. In 1784, having returned the Lord Lieutenant's secretary for his borough, he applied for advancement to an earldom. His application was not well received: Thomas Orde, Chief Secretary to the Lord Lieutenant said, "I shall preach with great energy against making any Irish peers on this side of the water. The enclosed letter from Lord Leitrim is in a style of menace which must not be allowed to succeed."

Robert submitted that he had brought more supporters to the government "without the smallest favour granted them" and thought he would surely win the King's favour after increasing the army presence in County Cavan (at considerable personal expense. This latter was recognised with an appointment to the role of Commissioner of the Revenue. The role however, lasted only a year. In a fit of pique, Robert declined to be compensated with the offer of an annual pension of £600. Instead, he demonstrated his continued support for succeeding Lord Lieutenants, doggedly petitioning each one with his application to be granted a higher title.

In the end, he had to wait ten years before being made a Viscount and another two years, until 1795, before being finally rewarded with the title Earl of Leitrim. The ultimate recognition had come after he played a key role in ensuring the successful election of the Lord Lieutenant's Secretary to Parliament. One of Robert's first accomplishments as Earl of Leitrim was to create the family seal and coat of arms. The motto he selected was Patriis Virtutibus: By Hereditary Virtues[13].

Having enjoyed the title for nine years, Robert died at the age of 72, no doubt satisfied with his life's work. In his later years, he found it less necessary to play the political game and compromise his personal views. Once he had achieved his goal of an earldom, he tied himself less to the influencers of the day and allowed his personal views to dictate his allegiances. At the end, he was a strong supporter of the Union of Great Britain and Ireland.

---

[13] The motto is taken from the Fourth Eclogue (a short pastoral poem) by the Roman poet Virgil, in praise of the emperor Augustus. The phrase means literally "By means of one's inherited virtues", and so describes a family whose achievements have depended on virtues passed from one generation to the next.

LEITRIM.

PATRIIS VIRTUTIBUS

Fig. 10: Leitrim coat of arms

Nathaniel Clements, 2nd Earl of Leitrim 1768-1854

Nathaniel Clements inherited the title of 2nd Earl of Leitrim and the Lough Rynn estate on the death of his father in 1804. Nathaniel divided his time between Dublin, London and his main residence at Killadoon, County Kildare. He maintained a close interest in Lough Rynn's affairs but only visited there occasionally and rarely for a long period. He did spend more time there once his son Robert took over the management of the estate. One of his more protracted visits was to lend support to his son when the 20 year old Robert fought the election (successfully) to take his father's seat as MP for Leitrim.

Nathaniel had an active political and social life and was prominent in both capitals. He was also well connected: he went to school with Arthur Wellesley, later Duke of Wellington, who remained a regular visitor to his home. He was also a close associate of the Prince of Wales.

Fig. 11: Nathaniel 2nd Earl of Leitrim

Clement, Percival Wood, 1937

Fig. 12: Mary, Countess of Leitrim, wife of the 2nd Earl of Leitrim

Both portraits painted by Sir Thomas Lawrence

By all accounts the 2nd Earl was a family man and had a wide circle of friends. He married Mary Bermingham, a noted beauty and joint heiress with her sister, Lady Charlemont, to the Rosshill Estate in Galway. When in London, the couple's centrally-located home at 2 Grosvenor Square was the base for many soirées and parties.

The Earl and his Countess had eight children and enjoyed an intimate family life. Siblings and parents all wrote regular, almost daily letters to each other when they were apart. These letters reflect a close relationship between the Earl and his Countess and between both parents and their children. The girls especially display an affectionate relationship with their father, addressing him in their letters as "dear Squeddles". The tone of the letters is unusual for the time; very informal and conversational and full of anecdotes of their daily lives. The Countess' letters to her husband bring him up-to-date on all the children's activities and especially their minor illnesses and ailments: the appearance of Sydney's fifth tooth when he was a year old warrants a detailed description. And all the letters express her wish for her husband's speedy return. The Earl in turn made it clear that he was grateful for "the uniform affectionate attachment which my wife has ever shown to me and by which she has rendered me the happiest of men".

The family travelled frequently, sometimes to relatives and sometimes abroad. The Earl was keen to provide his family with a well-rounded education. One of the children, Caroline, kept a journal of the family's six-month stay in Paris between 1815–'16, very soon after Duke of Wellington's victory over

Napoleon at Waterloo. Caroline records the family's concern for the Duke who was a family friend, and their pleasure when he made time to visit them at their apartments at Place Vendôme. The journal acknowledges some of the distress and upheaval of Paris after the war, recording the sight of beggars and injured soldiers filling the streets. However, most entries are detailed accounts of family visits to the Louvre, shopping excursions and parties. The Clements also held frequent prayer groups at their home for small groups of friends. Caroline notes one visit from "Uncle Robert", who, she was pleased to see, "is very well and does not feel any bad effects from the wound he received at the Waterloo". Her brothers, Robert and Sydney, the two elder sons and later owners of Lough Rynn, were left behind at boarding school in England. When she did meet up with him back in London, she remarked that Sydney (later Lord Leitrim), "looked very well". Incidentally, Caroline was the only sibling who retained any sort of positive relationship with Sydney in later life.

As a politician, the 2nd Earl was an active parliamentarian and liberal activist. He was Deputy Vice Treasurer and Teller of the Irish Exchequer and Member of Parliament for Leitrim from 1797–1804. On inheriting the earldom, he took his seat in the House of Lords. Nathaniel was a passionate politician, but had little time for the internal politicking in Parliament. He was vocal in his disapproval of the many offices and jobs conferred on politicians for which they gained income but did minimal work. And he was not altogether approving of administrative positions being passed from father to son: he resigned the post of Searcher, Packer and Gauger when it devolved to him from his brother. He was favoured by the infamous and profligate Prince Regent—at least up until 1809. Apparently the Prince felt snubbed and withdrew his support when the Earl failed to attend a party thrown by the Lord Lieutenant that year.

In Parliament, the Earl sat with the Whigs[14] who were the most disposed to land reforms and tenants' rights. But even among his Liberal colleagues, Nathaniel held some of the most radical views, many of which were distinctly ahead of his time. He opposed the Act of Union in 1801—despite pressure from his father and the offer of a peerage from the government—and urged land and tenant reforms beyond those proposed by his party. He set himself apart from his peers by considering himself Irish, and implored his heirs to do the same. In 1821 he wrote:

> I hope that (my heir) will ever consider himself an Irishman and that he will not adopt the very contemptible modern fashion of looking down upon his country. . . . He should recollect that he never can be of consequence or even respectable in England unless he is respectable in Ireland.

---

[14] In Parliament, the Whigs represented financial and mercantile interests (though their leadership was aristocratic), while the Tories represented the old landed interests that opposed the growing middle classes. Between 1830 and 1841, under the leadership of Earl Grey and Lord John Russell, the Whigs put through a great deal of reforming legislation including the 1834 Poor Law Amendment Act and the subsequent 1838 Irish Poor Law.

> (Should he get elected to Parliament) he will connect himself with men of strict constitutional principles of like, enlightened and disinterested views but above all with men that are friends to Ireland. *(2nd Earl's underlining.)*

In his Will, the Earl left his library of books relating to Irish history and Irish affairs as an heirloom to the title. He believed it to be "both his interest and his duty to have at least his country residence in Ireland, to visit his estates as often as he conveniently can to attend to the wants and interests of his tenantry and to cultivate their attachment and good opinion".

Nathaniel was a patron of music. In 1809, he helped to promote the 'Irish Harp Society of Ireland' whose aim was to "revive the native music and poetry of Ireland". It is not improbable that he was influenced by the knowledge that the famous harpist, Turlough O'Carolan, had lived only a few miles from Lough Rynn.

The Earl was in favour of education and sponsored five schools for children on the Lough Rynn estate: he donated the sites for the schoolhouses and gave each an annual donation of £10. In turn, his tenants back at Lough Rynn saw him as a man of honour and integrity, whose word was as good as his deed.

In the early 1820s, Ireland suffered greatly from famine and the Earl's income from his estates diminished rapidly[15]. He described his own circumstances as "poor and impoverished [though] not quite in a starving condition". He felt forced to take his family abroad, this time for economic rather than educational reasons.

He was gravely concerned about the effect the famine would have generally. He expressed his heartbreak at the reports he was getting of the terrible hardship and was "very anxious" to contribute to the General Fund. It was his expressed belief that it was "certainly the duty of everyone as far as their means will enable them to endeavour to relieve their fellow creatures in a time of such general distress".

During the Great Famine of the mid-1840s he maintained his liberal views, even when faced with rising levels of political crime and agitation on his own estates. And he placed blame for much of the distress on the government. He did, however, see some benefit in the amount of money being raised in England for the relief effort; it would, he hoped, make the Irish think more kindly of the English and be more accepting of their rule.

[15] The first major failure of the potato crop occurred in 1816 when Peel, (later Prime Minister) was Chief Secretary for Ireland. The crop failed again in 1817 causing a near-famine which was accompanied by an outbreak of typhus. Further serious food shortages occurred between 1822 and 1826.

The 2nd Earl, for all his liberal views and donations, did little of a practical nature to improve the land at Rynn and alleviate the lot of the tenants there. His relationship with the estate was distant and theoretical. It was left to Robert Bermingham Clements, the 2nd Earl's heir, to be the first resident landlord at Lough Rynn and to bring the estate into the 19th century. After him, it was the turn of his brother, Sydney, who would become the notorious 3rd Earl of Leitrim, Lord Leitrim.

Robert, Viscount Clements 1805-1839

The 2nd Earl of Leitrim, while retaining an interest in Lough Rynn, was happy to leave the management of the estate to his eldest son Robert, and later to a younger son, Sydney.

In 1833, at the age of 28, Robert Bermingham Clements moved to his newly-built manor house on the shores of Lough Rynn. The house would become known as Lough Rynn Castle but in fact was a relatively modest, two-storey house in a Tudor-revival style. Robert's primary concern lay with husbandry of the land, and he immediately set about improving farming methods on the estate. He shared the view of many that the explosive population growth and over-reliance on the potato would ultimately bring disaster. At this time, some 1,600 people lived in the town of Mohill, the nearest town to Lough Rynn; another 16,664 people lived in its environs. A major proportion (some 75%) of that population comprised families of poor labourers who relied on casual labour from small farms and who lived a wretched existence. Indeed life for most people in the area revolved around subsistence farming with few extra comforts. A quarter of the population comprised bigger farmers, professionals and merchants. They were more prosperous and were quite well served by the town of Mohill. Mohill, according to Samuel Lewis in 1837, was a "neatly built" town of 305 houses with the market on Thursday being "well supplied with grain and provisions of every kind". There was a local dispensary that offered medical assistance and a loan fund with capital of £300. Schools were dotted around the area: seven hundred children were taught in the eight public schools (five of which were sponsored by the 2nd Earl); a further nine hundred were taught in fifteen private schools. But not much of a community spirit was evident: in the same year that Robert Clements built his new home, an appeal was issued to the surrounding communities to ease the effects of the "present and impending danger" of cholera. The charity hoped to raise £150 to ease the plight of the suffering: "none whatsoever" was raised in Cloone; Mohill managed to contribute £30.

At the age of 20, Robert Clements had taken his father's parliamentary seat and proved to be an active parliamentarian and agrarian reformer: he was considered to be one of the leading members of the Irish Whigs at Westminster. He demonstrated a considerable intellect and wide-ranging interests in a book he wrote on Irish Agriculture and Poor Law. Robert combined his father's political outlook with a resolve to do something about the state of the land. He supported the 2nd Earl's view that it was the sacred duty of a landowner to live on his property, give employment and see to the welfare of the people. And he put his political and agricultural beliefs into practice: he introduced modern methods of farming and kept a close eye on his tenants.

Agricultural experts were brought in from England and Scotland to instruct the tenant farmers in new methods. Surveys were undertaken and main drainage works were carried out. New breeds of cattle were imported and new crops experimented with.

Robert's "exertions to improve the land, which had hitherto been much neglected" are recognised by Lewis, but observations on the condition of the estate by the Clements' indicate that much was yet to be done. Notes written by Robert and his father in 1838 show the sense of the annoyance and frustration felt by the landlords about the reluctance of the tenants to participate in the improvements. There are frequent suggestions that the tenants should be "spoken stiffly to"; eviction was proposed for errant and uncooperative tenants such as those in Drumdoo and Errew. Of others they wrote:

> "Anaghderg: There seems to be nothing done here lately. This is much to be regretted as the Morans began very well. I hope that Mr. Norris will explain to them that no indulgence can be given unless they exert themselves <u>more</u> to improve the land.
>
> Cloonclare: This is in a most wretched state. I do not know what we can do here but I am quite sure we are wrong in not trying <u>something</u>.
>
> Currycramp: The tenants here promise so well . . . should rebuild one of the houses and insist upon the farmers making their cottiers' houses less

> discreditable. (We should) eject cottiers sitting rent-free immediately and let them make what bargain they please for a new house elsewhere . . . (I) do not want to throw them off the estate or townland but break off their free rights."

In many ways, Robert was fighting a losing battle. The tenantry had reason to be suspicious of a reforming landlord and were loathe to hand over control to a new arrival, especially having been left to their own devices for many years. These people were not used to anybody directing their actions and remained locked in traditional ways and values, more so than in other parts of the country. They listened to no-one, except perhaps for the local priest. Priests had power, not necessarily because of their religious authority, but rather because they were accorded near mystical power by a people who believed far more in fairies, magical cures, changelings and curses than in Catholic doctrine. They were also isolated from many national events: one traveller to Leitrim at this time remarked that he met few people who had heard of the Catholic Emancipation movement. This major national issue dominated social and political life across most of the country but seemed to have barely touched parts of County Leitrim.

In any case, at Lough Rynn, Robert Clements did not live long enough to see most of his plans through. He suffered all his life from lung trouble—which may have been tuberculosis—and died from a severe cold when he was 33.

William Sydney Clements: 3rd Earl of Leitrim 1806-1878

When Robert died in 1839, management of the Lough Rynn estate and the title Viscount Clements passed to his brother William Sydney Clements. For the next fifteen years, Sydney, Viscount Clements managed the estate on behalf of his father only taking ownership on the death of the 2nd Earl in 1854. Sydney is the most notorious of all the residents of Lough Rynn Castle and is remembered mostly for callous and merciless acts against tenants. But at the beginning he continued the work he and his brother had started and was perceived as "a just and generous man and of benevolent disposition". It was only later, after he became the 3rd Earl, that he began to earn his reputation as a ruthless landlord and pitiless evictor.

As a younger son, Sydney had never expected to inherit the title or the lands. From what little we know of his early life, it appears that he was raised in a loving home by doting parents and participated in family activities with his seven siblings. But even as a child, he showed early signs of the man he would become.

Fig. 13: William Sydney Clements, 3rd Earl of Leitrim

Unlike his brother Robert, Sydney was neither a dutiful son nor a model student. He quarrelled with his brothers, ignored homework set for school holidays, and his letters lack the affectionate informality and day-to-day trivia that characterise correspondence between his other siblings and parents.

After attending private schools in England, first at Ham, then Beaconsfield, Sydney followed the route of many younger sons and joined the army. At seventeen, he entered the military academy at Sandhurst and graduated three years later. After graduation, he joined the 43rd Light Infantry and did tours of duty in Gibraltar and Portugal. Sydney was the epitome of the dashing, hot-tempered young soldier. He was tall and imposing and renowned for his physical strength and stamina. His letters home are full of his growing arrogance and self-importance. They demonstrate his fascination with the glories and the detail of the campaigns and reject with utter boredom his mother's fervent piety and anxiety about his physical and spiritual health.

When not on army duty, Sydney spent much of his time in London, socialising and visiting his clubs. His lodgings were in Cork Street, right in the centre of Mayfair. He was a member of the Reform Club and Brooks, which says much about his political allegiances and social preferences. The Reform Club was the Gentlemen's Club for liberals in the 19th century: its members promoted reform in government and land ownership and were active in pushing the 1832 Reform Act through Parliament. (The Reform Club is also where the Jules Verne hero Phileas Fogg accepted the challenge to travel 'Around the world in 80 Days'.)

Sydney's active service career was relatively distinguished but short. Within five years he had risen to the rank of Captain but at age 24, while stationed in Lancashire, he badly injured his knee when a horse fell on him. He never fully recovered and suffered constant pain for the rest of his life. In 1835, he was placed on half-pay and forced to retire from his regiment. His consolation prize was an appointment as Aide-de-Camp to the Lord Lieutenant of Ireland.

> ***Bills***
>
> *Rent of house in Cork St. £5/10/9*
>
> *Reform Club subs. £7/7/0*
>
> *Brooks Club subs. £12/12/0*
>
> *Horses £18/10 + £15/12*
>
> *Whip 12/6*
>
> *Hatter £1/8*
>
> *Boots £4*
>
> *Watchmaker £3/5*
>
> *Cigars £5/5/6*

As a 29 year old, retired army Captain, Sydney had a salary of £211/7/11[16] a year, which would have been the minimum needed to maintain his upper-class lifestyle. Luckily for him, he could also rely on allowances from his father plus interest from funds in his name, bringing him a total income of nearly £500 a year. This was, on occasion, further augmented by generous gifts: an entry in Sydney's personal accounts lists a present of £100 from his father and £50 from his mother "on going abroad". By 1840 (and after the death of his brother) Sydney's allowance had increased seven-fold. Out of this he paid subscriptions to his gentlemen's clubs and

---

[16] In 'old' money, there were twenty shillings in a pound and twelve pence in a shilling. A sum is written £/s/d: e.g. ten pounds, six shillings and eight pence is £10/6/8. In Euro, 1 shilling (1/-) is equal to about 6.3cent and 1d is ½cent; £1 would be equivalent to 79c. Older readers may like to consider that €1 = 15s/9d.

numerous other bills, including necessary accessories like a whip, boots, watch and hats. Sydney was evidently fond of a good cigar (despite imposing a ban on smoking on the estate in later years): his spending on cigars almost equalled the rent he paid on a house in Cork Street. His biggest bill of all was for his horses for which he paid nearly £34.

When in Ireland, Sydney worked on the family's estates and displayed an early interest in agriculture. A letter written by him to the editor of the Edinburgh Review in April 1836 reflects his interests and his character. In his letter, Sydney takes the writer of "an otherwise excellent article" to task for making little reference to the state of agriculture in Ireland. He writes to enquire whether there might be place in a future issue for a short paper on the subject and encloses some "observations with which the subject might be introduced". He shows himself to be up-to-date and knowledgeable about progressive farming techniques suggested by Mr. Black in a recent pamphlet.

> "Whether it is in my power to treat it in such a way as to merit a place in that journal, is a matter for your consideration, when the paper shall be finished, - but I have wished to inquire before I proceed to put my ideas together in that particular shape whether you think the question is too local to admit being made a matter of interest to your readers. . . . . . I should ask therefore to review the agricultural part of the Commissioner's appendix and show by a reference to it and to other facts, the great probability of an indefinite increase of

> exports from Ireland, by the extension of Mr Black's system."

The letter gives some indication of Sydney's arrogance: while he lauds the potential of Mr. Black's system to increase Irish exports, he also dismisses it as "nothing but the ordinary theory of farming, reduced to that small scale, which we in Ireland are so unfortunately brought to".

He spent a good deal of time at Lough Rynn and partnered his brother in managing the estates. The two brothers shared intellectual interests: both followed their father's Whig party and both were students of agricultural economics. They belonged to a group known as 'Improvers' that sought to improve agricultural techniques and expand the scope of agriculture.

Taking over at Lough Rynn

Robert's early death in 1839 was a blow to the whole family, but it paved the way for the new Lord Clements to take full control of the estate and impose his own personal management style.

At first he modelled himself on his brother and father and won admiration and respect from tenants and peers for his diligence and dedication to improving the estates. He continued in the family's political footsteps and won the parliamentary by-election caused by his brother's death.

But as time went on, the daring, rash young soldier became a proud, imperious landlord with a hasty temper which he indulged more and more over the years. In early years, he was more able to control it—or avoid occasions where he thought he might lose it. He was known to send his steward to deal with an issue he should have dealt with personally, saying he did not trust himself to control his temper. Few escaped being the object of vindictive action or petty retaliation and tenants, peers and the administration in Dublin were held equally in contempt. Sydney seems to have lived exclusively for work: he never married and spent much of his time travelling around his estates checking on tenants and managing the minutiae of his affairs. His journals, account books and rent ledgers are testimony to his obsessive attention to detail. While many of his ideas were far-sighted, his autocratic tendencies and his belief in his own omnipotence created antagonism and rancour amongst most of the people he came in contact with; not least his tenants. His opinions and ideas were mostly rational and well thought through—but were intractable. Essentially, as one contemporary writer observed, he "was not a bad man—if he got his own way".

But things were changing for Sydney and his ascendancy peers. During the 250 years that the landlord class controlled this part of Ireland, there were few periods where they did not have to deal with some level of insurgence or rebellion. But throughout, they had been able to rely on the unqualified support of the English government. By the mid-1800s this had changed, and there was a visible shift in the relationship between the English and Irish ascendancy classes. The Act of Union in 1800 compounded this shift and heralded the gradual and complete erosion of the administrative, economic and political power of the landlords. Not only were they subject to increasing insurgence from their tenants, but they were increasingly seen as an unwanted problem by the English government. Or in the words of Marcus Clements[17], "the Irish squirearchy were reduced from the ruling elite of a semi-independent state of high civilization and culture to provincial country bumpkins in the Imperial Parliament in Westminster". In the 1840s, this change was becoming apparent in the way the parliament dealt with Ireland, using 'coercion' and repression rather than conciliation, and treating the Irish with a good deal less civility than the English. Viscount Clements was an active parliamentarian, sharing many of his father's liberal views and taking a seat for the Whigs. He worked with the radical Catholic politician, William Smith O'Brien, to try to push through administrative and agrarian reforms and was often chief spokesman for the Irish members during debates. But his antipathy towards authority of any kind led him to cross swords continuously with the Tory administration in Dublin Castle, with Parliament and with the Royal Irish Constabulary. His main battles with the administration were over Irish Coercion Bills, the standard government response to the most minor hint of disturbance in Ireland. Coercion generally resulted in increased police activity and sometimes forceful attempts to remove arms from the hands of Catholics. The Whigs (and Lord Clements) promoted a more conciliatory approach: they felt that brute force and intimidation could never result in a

---

[17] Marcus Clements, a second cousin twice removed of the 3rd Earl of Leitrim, was the last of the Clements family to live at Lough Rynn Castle.

lasting peace and would at best deliver short-term gains. At times, Clements was driven to take his grievances directly to the Prime Minister.

In October 1844, the government had responded to a series of disturbances with one of their many Coercion Bills. A letter from Clements to the British Prime Minister, Sir Robert Peel gives some insight into Sydney's attitude to the authorities; it also probably reflects the growing disrespect and disregard for the Irish Ascendancy by the English administration. The letter describes a call by the police to Lough Rynn and other homes for the purpose of taking down the names of the 'inmates'. First, Clements was outraged that the Police should be able to enter a house at will and ask for any information. He was positively apoplectic that the Inspector General of Police effectively dismissed his complaint and, far from apologising, suggested that they would just be more covert about it in the future. This letter is quite typical of Clements' style: it is long-winded, indignant and outraged. And it is written directly to the Prime Minister. It is however, worth reflecting on: for the Constabulary to act with such impunity must have felt like a huge imposition for Sydney, who calls on Peel to imagine how he would feel if he were subject to such an intrusion, or whether it would be permissible in England:

> I have been taught to believe that every Man's House, however humble is his Castle, and that no person has any right to enter it without a sufficient warrant for that purpose. I have also learned to have a lively horror of an Inquisition.

My house has been entered by a Police Man, for the purpose of taking down and writing the names of the inmates.

I enquired from his Officer what Authority he had for such an Act, he informs me that he had a "Confidential" communication from the Inspector General of Police, and declined to give me any further information but admitted that it was under his immediate orders that the sanctity of my roof has been violated. I have applied to the Inspector General of Police for his authority for this outrage and the only redress which he proposes to me is (as you will see by the enclosed copy of his letter) that for the future his espionage shall not be conducted so openly, but in a more secret form . . . not by "formal visits" but that the required information should be gathered incidentally.

I ask you, Sir, as an English Gentleman and Her Majesty's Prime Minister, if you would not be satisfied with such an answer, would you like Police Men of all sorts of characters to be instructed to acquire information to be "gathered incidentally" respecting the inmates of your House, would you be content that such enquiries should be made of the issues and characters of every inmate who may be present, or shall hereafter enquiry your Hospitality —if there can exist any Hospitality where such a system can be tolerated?

I was told two days ago by a most worthy and Excellent Gentleman of this neighbourhood who has a large family of Daughters, of whom he is justly proud, that when a Police Man called at his House for the names of the inmates, that it made his Heart bleed to write down all of his Dear Children's names to be bandied about by the Police in their Barracks, but that he thought that they had the Authority, and he complied, and it would make your heart bleed that if every honourable man to know that he is subject to such a system of Espionage, no matter how highly his Character be esteemed by those who know him.

I do not want to prejudge any case, but is it wonderful that such horrors should occur as are at present under investigation in Dublin, when the Inspector General of Police himself mistrusts Officers and their under his command to neglect their duties as Constables and to become Spies in their Districts, such a system is not only dangerous to individual Character, Happiness and Liberty, but subversive of the peace and well-being of the Country.

I have the honor to be

Your Most Obedient Serv[t] Clements

Peel's response offered little solace: he reminded Sydney that the Inspector General of Police in Ireland did not act under his (Peel's) direction and that he would forward the letter to the Lord Lieutenant of Ireland. Clements, typically, responds to Peel with barely restrained frustration:

> "Lord Clements regrets that his communication to Sir Robert Peel has been so fruitless. He did not write to Sir Robert Peel for the purpose of giving him trouble, but in the vain hope that . . . an act of abuse of power might be remedied."

(The other thing that is notable about this correspondence is the speed at which it was managed. The letters had to go between Lough Rynn and London and through whatever bureaucracy existed in both places. Yet Clements's first letter, written on 5th October, was replied to by Peel three days later on 8th October. Clements's response to Peel's letter was written on 14th October, only five days later.) Clements antagonism towards the government eventually came to a head during the famine which Clements blamed on the bureaucratic bungling of the government. He lost faith and interest in constitutional politics and retired as an MP in 1847 passing his seat to his brother Charles.

When he was not dealing with the bungling of an inept administration, Clements was obsessed with turning Lough Rynn into a model estate. He started by adding more outbuildings, including a coach house, stables, dairy and stores. He had a flair for architecture—no doubt inherited from his great-grandfather—and many of the constructions were built to his own design; incidentally, these buildings hardly reflect an austere and severe personality, being in a rather fanciful and picturesque style. He also had an eye for detail: his note-books record meticulous calculations for all aspects of the estate. For example, the plans to build a house at Treanmore included the following calculations:

> For 170 Perches of Masonry, including all
> Brick Work @ 35 cwt per perch 330 Tons
>
> For Carting the above 330 Tons as follows:
> Calculating that 2/3 of the quantity are drawn
> from the East side of Tryne that is 220 tons at
> 10 per Ton, each Horse supposed to bring 3½
> Tons per day in 12 Loads £9 : 3 : 4
>
> For Carting 1/3 of the quantity from the River
> on the West of Robt Cootes Farm, 8 Loads per
> day of 15 cwt each Load. 6 Tons per day
> 110 Tons @ £2 : 15 : 0
>
> £11 : 18 : 4

He also employed some of the leading architects of the day and brought in expert tradesmen and stone masons from as far away as London. The Estate Office was constructed in the 1850s to a design of Digby Wyatt, an architect who was also responsible for the Senate Chambers in Leinster House. He installed systems and contraptions to improve efficiency in various parts of the estate. A modern and ingenious water system was devised to bring water from the river just below Red Bridge (a couple of hundred metres from the Castle). The water was filtered as it flowed through a gravel-filled channel to the middle of the kitchen yard from where it was pumped up to large tanks on the roof of the house. The pump was operated by a horse circling it, led by a young boy.

A white marker attached to a ball-cock would appear, signalling that the tanks were full. Similarly, the lime-kiln built at Farnaught was unique in Ireland: it produced lime of a very rare high quality and was used in all the houses on the estate. Throughout the estate Clements planted a range of trees, including many unusual ones imported from abroad[18]. Such was the level of production that lumber from Lough Rynn was exported to Britain and Europe and the saw-mill played a central role in the economy of the estate. But while he could see the commercial value of lumber, Clements cared passionately about trees and indeed seemed to accord them a consideration rarely encountered by the people around him. Goats were banned because of the damage they did to trees and any that were found on his land were ordered to be killed. Tenants needed his personal permission to cut any wood, including bushes for cleaning chimneys and ash (which was commonly used for various tools). He appeared genuine in his desire to avoid wilful destruction of a tree, likening it to "bleeding the poor bush" or having one's fingers cut off. And his belief extended to dead trees: he forbad the retrieval of bog-oak on the estate. Clements' interest extend-ed to horticulture and he built one of the most technically-advanced glasshouses of the day. It was oriented to create a benign micro-climate that allowed a huge range of fruit and vegetables to be grown.

---

[18] Many of these trees still stand. The Tree Council of Ireland lists Lough Rynn as home to 13 'champion' trees including Leitrim's tallest, a Sequoia-dendron giganteum (Wellingtonia, Giant Sequoia) that stands at 5.69m × 36.50m.

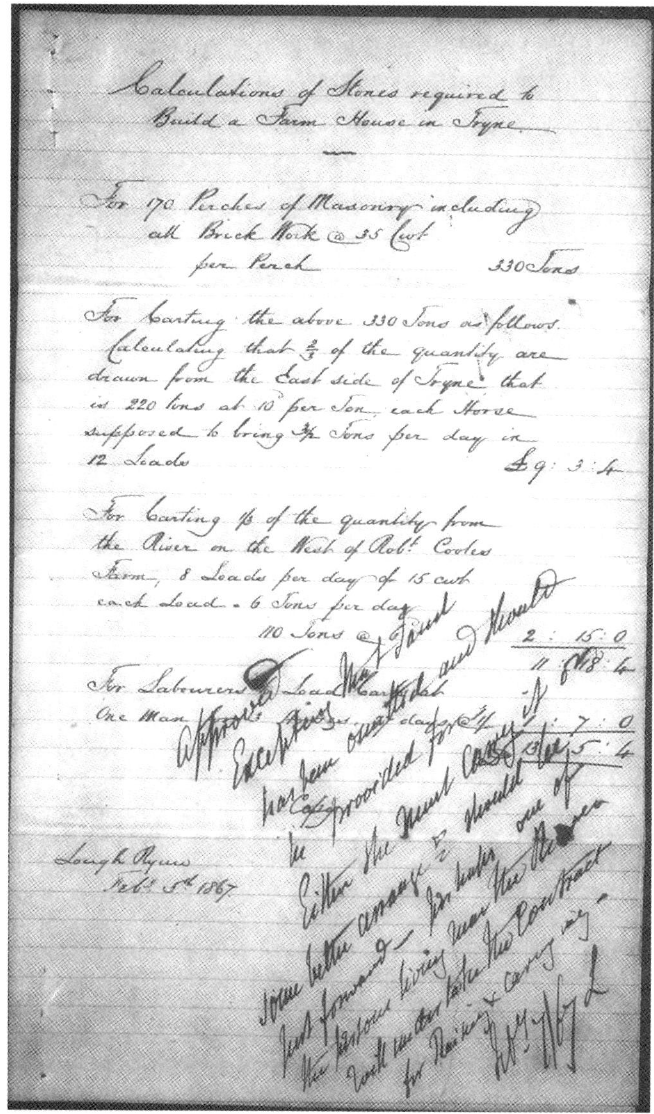

Calculations of Stones required to Build a Farm House in Tryne

For 170 Perches of Masonry including all Brick Work @ 35 Cwt per Perch — 330 Tons

For Carting the above 330 Tons as follows. Calculating that 2/3 of the quantity are drawn from the East side of Tryne that is 220 tons at 10d per Ton, each Horse supposed to bring 3½ Tons per day in 12 Loads — £9 : 3 : 4

For Carting 1/3 of the quantity from the River on the West of Robt Cooles Farm, 8 Loads per day of 15 cwt each Load - 6 Tons per day 110 Tons @ [illegible] — 2 : 15 : 0

[illegible] : 4

For Labourers to Load the Carts [illegible] One Man [illegible] days @ 1/ — [illegible] : 7 : 0

[illegible] : 5 : 4

Lough Rynn
Feby 5th 1867

Approved [illegible]

Fig. 14: Notes from the Leitrim Estate regarding building requirements

The walled gardens at Lough Rynn covered over an acre and were designed by leading architects, Deane & Woodward. They were augmented with imported soil and planted with imported plants in the fashion of the day, including rhododendrons, azaleas, monkey puzzle trees, fuchsia and exotic grasses. At the end of the walled gardens, a quite romantic folly was built in 1867. Again designed by Deane & Woodward, its only function was to offer a beautiful sanctuary from which one could enjoy an uninterrupted view of the lake.

Given his interest in agricultural advances, it is not surprising that Clements followed a national fashion and founded, in January 1844, the South Leitrim Agricultural Society. The aim of the Society was to improve agricultural practices and land management. It set out to "benefit the agricultural interests in this County and to ameliorate the condition of all classes of farmers or those interested in the increase of the produce of the soil by affording information, encouraging an improved system of husbandry and the introduction of a better description of stock and farming implements." The first Agricultural Show was held in the same year and prizes were given for crops and animals and produce from cottage gardens. Especially valuable prizes were awarded for crops such as turnips and clover which were uncommon but highly approved of by the agricultural reformers. The Society's annual dinner was held in the coach house and was attended by all the local gentry and committee members.

Apart from the building and horticultural work, Clements undertook major land reclamation and outlawed the burning of land and the 'rundale' system of farming. Under the rundale system, families pooled resources to rent land, and were each allocated a piece proportional to their individual contribution. Over the years, the pieces of land became smaller and smaller as each family continued to sub-divide their plot. What was left would frequently be inadequate to support a family. Theophilus Jones, a local Mohill farmer put it succinctly: "If a man thinks he is near death and he has six acres and three sons, he will give them two acres apiece and they will do the same so that the holding is dwindled away to a cabbage garden." Clements predicted that this system would lead to major problems and indeed, the devastation of the Famine was exacerbated by tenants left operating farms too small to sustain even one family.

And the tenants were not helped by the quality of the land in the area: it was poor, boggy and lacked nutrients as a result of poor land management. And the climate was frequently cold and damp.

Samuel Lewis, in his Topographical Dictionary of Ireland in 1842, describes the land and the state of agriculture in the area. The land, Lewis noted, was poor and "exceedingly retentive of water"; Mohill was surrounded by "large tracts of deep dark rich loam on a limestone bottom". The land, he observed, was exhausted by excessive rotation of crops, was rarely manured and was left to "recruit itself" while being thoroughly infested with weeds; the main crops were oats, flax, a little bit of wheat and especially potatoes.

Fig. 15: The 'folly' at Lough Rynn

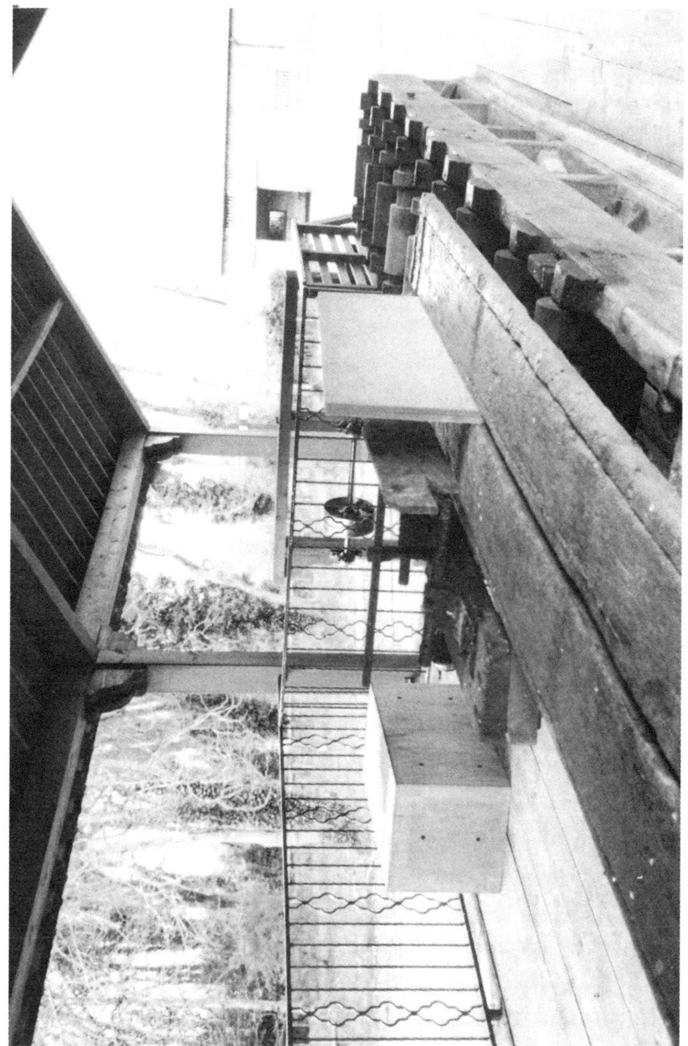

Fig. 16: The sawmill at Lough Rynn

The Rent Window,
through which
tenants paid their
rent and labourers
paid their wages

Fig. 17: The 'rent window' at Lough Rynn

Fig. 18: The yard bell and water pump at Lough Rynn

Lewis laments the fact that grass or clover was rarely sown, rendering the land almost useless until it became sown with potatoes again. He observed, however, that "even on the coarsest and most marshy soils", cows thrived, and "both milk and butter are of excellent flavour".

Life at Lough Rynn

The work day at Lough Rynn Castle was marked by the pealing of the yard bell: it was rung by the yardman at half past seven to start the day and again at midday to call lunch and a short rest period. The day finished at half past five. Everything needed to be done by hand and the workers were kept busy on jobs like planting or working in the stables or steaming potatoes for the pigs. Operators were also needed for farm machinery like the thresher and for the steam engine used to power the sawmill. While some were lucky enough to have permanent jobs that lasted through the year, much of the work on the estate (and on farms in general) was seasonal casual labour. Work was available largely in the spring for sowing and in the autumn for harvest, providing at most, five months of wage-earning months in the year. Outside of these months, the labourers endured long periods of unemployment. John Duke, the local physician in Mohill, described the labourers' situation as "wretched beyond anything I could say, both as to diet and accommodation".

It was this labouring class that would be most affected by the Great Famine. They had nothing. They existed season to season in tiny mud cabins on a patch of land that they leased under a system called 'conacre'. Under conacre, they were given a plot for a single season in exchange for casual labour and/or rent. They used the plot to grow enough potatoes to feed themselves and to keep a pig. Even when they got paid work, a labourer would often not make enough to feed his family or pay the rent, and the pig was frequently sold to meet his debts. For the labourers, this meant that they were totally dependent on their small potato crop and were never more than a step away from starvation. One bad night of blight would cause their sole food source to rot leaving them totally destitute.

Even before the Famine, the labourers were under threat. Many farmers were moving away from conacre and labour-intensive, crop-based agriculture to livestock farming which was more profitable and required less labour. This inevitably aggravated the underlying tension amongst the labourers, doing away, as it did, with both their homes and their livelihoods.

This was all acknowledged in a report to the Devonshire Commission in 1844 in which the authors seemed torn between supporting the system and condemning its frequently distressing outcomes. The Report noted:

> Much has been said in condemnation of this system; but still we are convinced that some practice of this nature is essential to the comfort, almost the existence, of the Irish peasant. Under ordinary circumstances the wages of his labour alone will not enable him to purchase food and other necessaries, and to pay even the most moderate rent. It becomes therefore necessary

> that he should resort to some other means for procuring subsistence, and these can only be found in the occupation of a piece of ground which shall furnish a crop of potatoes for food. Although the taker of con-acre ground may, in ordinary years, receive a good return for the rent which he assumes, yet, as the amount of such rent, although not unreasonable in respect of the farmer's expenditure upon the land, is always large with reference to the ordinary means of a labourer, a bad season, and a failure in the crops, leave the latter in a distressed condition, subject to a demand which he is wholly unable to meet."

Fig. 19: Extract from Report to the Devonshire Commission, 1844

For the labourers, there were few ways to rise above this hand-to-mouth existence, except perhaps by doing well at migrant work in Northern Ireland or Scotland (Leitrim had a much higher rate of migrant workers than other counties at 16 in 1,000). There was little solace at home: housing was poor, either small thatched cottages or one-roomed, window-less huts, barely twelve feet square, made of stone and turf and mud and roofed with branches and peat. The only furnishings inside might be a straw bed and a pot over a fire for cooking potatoes, with a hole in the roof to let the smoke out. Treats were rare. At Christmas (in the early years at least), Clements distributed meat amongst the families of the workers and held parties at the coach house for the children. The emerging agricultural and social landscape was noted by Lewis in 1842 in his description of the conditions under which people lived:

> "The farm houses are usually long narrow cabins, which sometimes shelter the cattle in common with the family; but houses of a better description, with chimneys, partitions and separate or detached buildings, are gradually superseding them. The fuel is everywhere turf, procured in great abundance through every part of the county. The general food is potatoes and oaten bread, sometimes with buttermilk or fish; butchers meat is only used at Easter and Christmas, or on other great festive occasions. The clothing of the men is neat and strong, the coat mostly of frieze, the small clothes of corduroy; the females mostly wear a coarse woollen stuff petticoat, and of late cotton gowns have become common. The general character of the people is that of sobriety and industry; the English language is everywhere spoken by adults and children, and mostly by elderly people, except in the remote mountain districts, and even there it rarely occurs that a person is met who cannot speak it."

Each week, the workers at Lough Rynn took their place on the 'pay seat' under a porch opposite the offices to wait for their wages. When it was their turn, they would stand on a block of cut stone to receive their pay through a tiny window near the door of the coach house (pictured in Fig. 17). They were paid on a Wednesday to enable them to go to the market or fair day in Mohill on Thursday. A man earned six pence for threshing and cleaning a barrel of oats (which later sold for up to 14 shillings at market); attending cattle or planting laurels would pay ten pence a day, while pulling turnips would get you only six pence. To put this in context, the wages for all workers on the Lough Rynn estate amounted to about £240 a year. In contrast, the local schoolmaster was paid £30 a year and the schoolmistress, £20; the master of Mohill workhouse was paid £50 plus rations and the nurse's salary was £8. And these were by no means the highest-paid professionals. On Market Day, the workers from Lough Rynn might go to Mohill to spend some of their hard-earned money: Main Street had "several good shops, well stocked with various articles of fashion and of local requisites". A man earning six to ten pence a day could easily spend it on a pint of stout and a single loaf of bread. While the labourer and small tenant families lived on a monotonous diet of potatoes and milk, relieved occasionally by a herring or bacon, life at the big house was different. The recipe books from Lough Rynn Castle show an interest in plain but varied food, with a decided preference for desserts and sweets. Much of the produce was grown in the greenhouse or imported. Oranges were particularly favoured, and were used in everything from marmalade to various types of pudding. Most of the recipes would not be unusual today. They include Onion Soup, Fricassee of Chicken, Indian Curry, Lobster Sauce, Almond Cheese Cakes, Apple Fritters, Waffles and Walnut 'Catchup'. The directions on 'How to

Shopping list

Tea (1lb) 2/8

Pint stout - /2

1 oz tobacco - /3

Bread (4 lb loaf) 0/8

Eggs (½ doz) 0/6

Castor oil (1 oz) 0/2

2 Lead pencils (std) 0/1

Dress a Boar's Head' may, however, have less pertinence for today's cook. The housekeeper's book of cures, tinctures and remedies includes treatments for a wide range of ailments including asthma (hyssop and honey), coughs, headaches, heartburn, worms, wind, and indigestion (rhubarb and ginger with a glass of wine after dinner). Insects may have been a problem: there are detailed instructions on how to destroy all sorts of bugs. And the housekeeper (or Lord Leitrim) was obviously meticulous about the linen: there are careful notes on how to clean white cloth.

Despite having had an active social life in London, Clements seemed to keep much more to himself when he was at Lough Rynn. Over the years he invited fewer and fewer visitors. The only regular guests were his agent or other neighbours who would join him for the occasional dinner, and his father, who visited relatively frequently until his death in 1854. He may have spent a little more time with one of his closest neighbours, Sir Morgan Crofton. Crofton was a fellow card-player, and the two apparently played for high stakes. In one game, Clements won Clooncahir House from his neighbour—a substantial residence just south of Mohill. (Crofton could probably afford it: in 1844, his income from his Mohill estates was £7,000.) Visits by his peers were rarer. One visit of note was by Lady Rossmore and her daughter, Norah. They stayed for more than a few days, apparently part of an attempt by Clements to play matchmaker between his nephew Robert and Norah. It did not work, and Robert's disinterest is believed to have been one of the reasons why Clements later disinherited him.

The Great Famine

Tenants and labourers across Leitrim experienced hard times in the 1830s and '40s. For those who relied on it, the potato crop yielded just enough to stave off starvation. In 1838, in response to the increasing levels of poverty, the Whig government decided to implement the English Poor Law in Ireland. The 'Poor Law' aimed to deal with poverty at local level by building and running 'workhouses' to house and feed the poor of the area. An important element of the Law was that it required the workhouses to be financed by local rates and to be administered locally by a Board of Guardians. The Board usually comprised local gentry, including landowners, clergy, well-off townspeople, wealthy farmers and traders of the area. The Board struck a 'poor rate' (payable by the same gentry) and ran the local workhouse on the proceeds. This worked relatively well when the government was augmenting funds raised, and when demand on funds was low. But it would prove a problem later when those same farmers and traders were handed full responsibility for the funding and administration of the large-scale relief required during the Famine.

As a reforming Whig, Clements was one of four Irish commissioners selected to implement the Poor Law throughout Ireland. The Order to set up Mohill Union was issued on 5th September 1839, with thirteen Electoral Divisions for electing Poor Law Guardians: Mohill, Eslin, Annaduff, Annaveagh, Rinn, Cloone, Aughavas, Carrigallen, Newtowngore, Drumreilly, Ballinamore, Oughteragh and Fenagh. Local Justices of the Peace were directed to meet at Mohill Court House on 16th September to appoint 'ex-officio' Guardians from their own ranks: they did so and the Board was duly elected with Clements as Chairman. In June 1840, the Union was directed to set a poor rate to cover part of the cost of the new workhouse. Two years later, on 8th June 1842, Mohill Workhouse opened its doors to the 'Destitute Poor'. It had cost nearly £8,000: £6,700 for the construction and the rest on furniture and fittings. It was located in Hyde Street and was typical of its kind: it covered over six acres and was designed to hold a maximum of 700 inmates (though the average number of inmates in the first three years was about 230). When it opened, it was neither a popular nor attractive option for the destitute: men, women, girls and boys were all housed in separate quarters and families might only be allowed to meet once a week; the day was regimented and anyone breaking the many rules suffered severe punishment. Food was poor and portions were small; bedding was uncomfortable and there was little to protect a body from the cold and damp. Many became ill. In 1844, a Fever Hospital was built to deal with the increasing incidence of Typhus and 'yellow' fever, but many died and were buried in mass 'paupers' grave' beside the Workhouse.

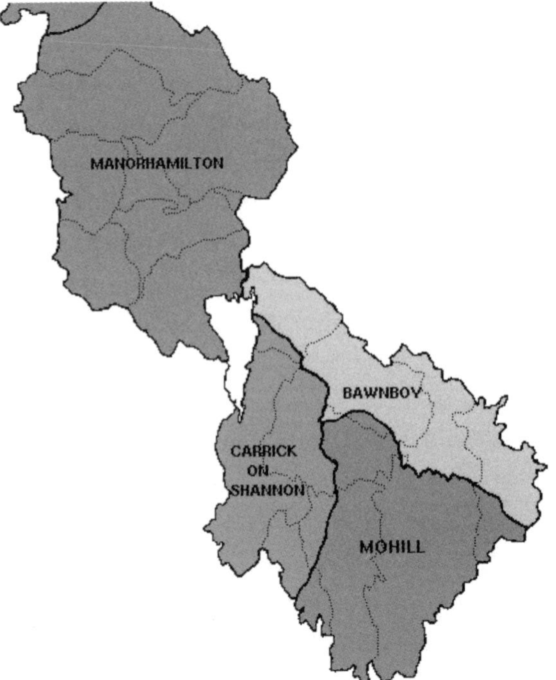

Fig. 20: Map showing Mohill Union

In 1845, there was optimism about the year's potato harvest. In August, at the annual Agricultural Society Dinner, Clements spoke confidently about the great progress that had been made in agriculture in Leitrim and expectations of an abundant potato crop were high. The few people who sounded warnings of a general failure of the potato crop were largely ignored. The naysayers were unfortunately right: the 1845 potato crop fell to a crippling blight and heralded what became known as the Great Hunger or Great Famine.

August 1845 was sunny and warm and the shiny healthy green stalks in every field gave hope for an abundant harvest. But on a single night, all changed. People woke up to see their previously healthy crops turned overnight into a mass of rotting weeds. The lucky ones had already harvested some of their crop but most were faced with a winter of hunger and destitution. By the early autumn of that year it was clear that famine was imminent across Ireland. The Conservative Prime Minister, Sir Robert Peel established a Scientific Commission to review the issue: it quickly concluded that over half of Ireland's potato crop might perish due to "'wet rot". Unfortunately, the report was published too late to have any effect. A temporary Relief Commission was established in November 1845 to advise the government on the extent of problem in Ireland and to oversee whatever national and local relief efforts that might be implemented. Local relief committees were established in February 1846 with a remit to help organize employment projects and distribute food to the poor. They would also raise money from landowners to cover part of the cost, with their funds being matched by the government. The committees were successful to a point, but were hampered by lack of understanding of local conditions and a determination to withhold much food relief until June, when, it was believed, there would be real hardship. The relief effort was overseen by Charles Edward Trevelyan[19]. In early 1846, he was appointed to implement a public works program for Ireland's destitute but his understaffed

[19] The same Trevelyan referred to in the frequently sung ballad, "The Fields of Athenry".

administration floundered in bureaucracy and had no capacity to deal with the level of requests for relief. Whatever his acknowledged intellectual brilliance, he was hardly an appropriate choice for a job that required a modicum of objectivity and compassion. In October, 1846, he called the Famine the "cure" to the overpopulation of Ireland that "has been applied by the direct stroke of an all-wise Providence in a manner as unexpected and as unthought of as it is likely to be effectual." Two years later he declared: "The great evil with which we have to contend is not the physical evil of the famine, but the moral evil of the selfish, perverse and turbulent character of the people." To augment the public works, Peel found funding for two shipments of inexpensive Indian corn (American maize) which would be sold cheaply to the poor in Ireland. The plan was for the Relief Commission to sell the meal at cost to local relief committees which in turn would sell it at cost to the Irish poor at a penny per pound. But the plan was ill-fated in more ways than one: the needy people had little money to buy the corn, and when they did, they found it difficult to cook, barely digestible, caused diarrhoea and, for a people used to the bulky potato, it hardly made for a satisfying meal.

Peel's single other effort was the repeal of the Corn Laws in May 1846. The Corn Laws had set artificially high and fluctuating prices for corn but their repeal and subsequent reduced prices brought little benefit. The problem for the Irish poor was less a lack of food than a lack of money with which to buy it. There was plenty of wheat, meat and dairy produce in Ireland but much of it was being exported to England and was certainly not being made available at reduced prices. And there was no appetite in government for giving food to the starving: it would only encourage what was believed to be endemic laziness amongst the Irish. Due in large part to removing the Laws and the price-protection, Peel was quickly embroiled in a political furore that ended with his resignation from office.

Peel was replaced in June 1846 by Lord John Russell and a Whig administration: Russell and his new administration quickly took liberalism and laissez-faire to extremes. The new government's first instinct was to reject any direct state intervention or aid and instead sought to leave the solution to the Irish themselves. Charles Wood, the new Chancellor of the Exchequer, justified the policy on the basis that "except through a purgatory of misery and starvation, I cannot see how Ireland is to emerge into anything approaching either quiet or prosperity".

As a consequence, the relief was restructured to emphasise public works the main source of help. More disastrously, the government, rigidly adhering to free-market principles, stopped the subsidised supplies of low-cost corn. Food prices fell to the natural laws of economics: supply was short and demand was high, and there was no competition from cheap imports. The corn merchants pushed the price beyond the means of the majority of the population. At the market in Mohill, the price of oatmeal doubled between 1845 and 1847; the price of potatoes increased four-fold.

Although the English administration signally failed to respond adequately to the crisis in Ireland, neither did the local farmers and large land-holders. Throughout the Famine, their lands were producing enough to feed and clothe the population twice over, yet Ireland continued to be a net exporter and sent £100,000 worth of food out of Ireland every month. The export of live cattle to Britain increased during the Famine, as did exports of bacon and ham.

Relief and public works

In Mohill, the Board of Mohill Union was struggling with internal as well as external issues: in January 1846, three of its worthy members, George Crofton, Edward Donnelly and James Moran were prosecuted for appropriating rates. In March, the Union reported that one-third of the potato crop was lost and "the distress of the population is great". On March 19th, the Board communicated their serious concerns to the Commissioners and called for works to provide the stricken people with a small income and a depot of cheap Indian meal to be both instituted forthwith.

In April, Clements was appointed by the Lord Lieutenant to set up local Relief Committees in Leitrim to oversee the provision of relief through a combination of charity and self-help. In typical style, Clements was dismissive of the Commission's 'Instructions to Committees of Relief'. The instructions to form a committee from resident gentry, main landholders and clergy were, he felt, "totally inapplicable" in a district where "landlords are almost unknown, the Rector of Cloone absent, and agents frequently non-resident".

His opinion of the Commission notwithstanding, Clements took his role seriously and instigated a number of 'works' around the area to provide employment and income for the poor. Most works involved road-building projects: in some cases, existing roads were improved; in others wholly new, and often quite superfluous, roads were built.

In March 1846, Clements organised a petition for public funding of an ambitious project to link Lough Erne and the River Shannon. The petition was signed by the "landed proprietors and magistrates and residents of the County of Leitrim", including Clements, High Sheriff La Touche, A. Lawder, Charles Cox, Robert Noble, B. Peyton, John Peyton, James B McKeon, James McTernan, Mrs K Little, James Armstrong, Alexander Knott, J. Peyton, James Nutley, Alex Perry, Crofton, Guy Lloyd. As well as being the first of the signatories, Clements wrote a supporting letter urging the government to fund "this Great National Work" to help alleviate "the extraordinary poverty of the locality". Clements went on to explain that the collectable Poor Rates in South Leitrim could never be adequate to relive their current distress and expressed his confidence that the petition would meet with "a warm desire on your [Peel's] part to relieve our distress".

The petition was successful: the Ballinamore-Ballyconnell canal was built between 1847 and 1860, with up to 7,000 men employed in its construction. It cost £228,651.[20]

---

[20] From 1860 to 1881, only eight boats paid the toll to use the canal and it was abandoned as a navigable waterway, but maintained for drainage. The canal was re-opened in 1994 and renamed the Shannon-Erne Waterway..

One practical scheme, already in planning, was expedited. The Rinn and Blackriver Drainage Scheme was designed to improve the land and reduce flooding in much of south Leitrim. Its chief designer was Thomas J. Mulvaney, the district officer of Belturbet Board of Works'. [21]

In 1846, the scheme was promoted and publicised: a description of the planned works[22] was posted in Mrs. Little's hotel in Mohill and notices were posted in surrounding townlands. The plan was to drain 4,097 acres (revised to 5,691 acres in 1851) at a cost of £23,392. By November 1846, the Board had the required consent of more than half of the landowners. Work commenced, and by July 1847 over 3,400 men were employed on the scheme. The work was designed ultimately to pay for itself with increased rents on the improved land, though landowners could object to rent increases if they felt their holding had not benefited.

---

[21] The drainage district was divided in three: the first covering the Rinn River, Lough Rynn, Lough Errew and the Lurga River. Also included was the Blackriver from the Rinn River to Bellantra bridge (just south of Farnaught). The second division consisted of the Cloone river and its tributaries; the third, the Blackriver above Bellantra.

[22] This scheme was one of many that was accelerated and facilitated by the Drainage (Ireland) Act of 1846. This dispensed with the need for private funding of preliminary expenses, and empowered the government to carry out the works under the direct control of the Board. The Act also reduced the need for landowners assent to the work. The Act led to an unprecedented level of drainage works throughout the country.

While the labourers toiled to avoid starvation, landholders continued to focus on their own concerns. John Kane of Mohill objected to a rent increase, claiming that the drains were insufficiently large and that a planned bridge had not been built, thus making access to his lands more difficult.

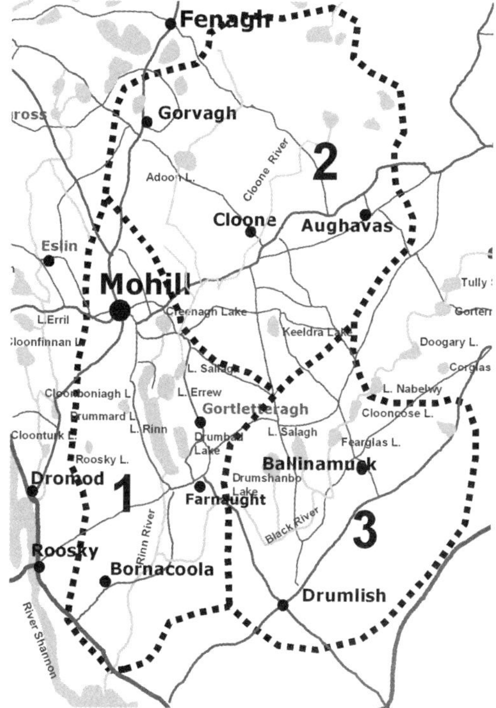

Fig. 21: Map showing the area covered by the Rinn and Blackriver Drainage Scheme

Sir George Crofton claimed that a weir at the outlet of Lough Rinn kept the water at an artificially high level and did not allow his lands to drain sufficiently. The owners of thirty-one eel weirs also claimed compensation for their losses.

Predictably, Viscount Clements also clashed with the Board. Though originally the main sponsor and promoter of the scheme, he wanted the original water level at Lough Rinn to be maintained. At one stage, the Board needed to lower the lake temporarily to facilitate on-going work below the lake on the Rinn River. Clements objected and barred officers of the Board from entering his property. Clements also complained vociferously to the site officers that a change in the course of the Rinn River had resulted in the loss of some of his land. Though the land in question amounted to less than an acre, the issue was escalated to the Secretary of the Board of Works; an arbitrator was appointed and a settlement of sixteen shillings was agreed.

Not all petitions for works were successful. A petition to fund public works from Clements to Peel on 24th May 1846 was summarily rejected and reflects the growing attitude of the government. Peel pushed responsibility for the relief firmly back to the Board: the petition was one, he replied, which should be dealt with locally by "Representatives of the District from which it proceeds". He also considered that the very presentation of a petition "of this nature" might be considered to imply passivity and inertia on the part of the petitioners and any interference on his part could only conflict with his duty as First Lord of the Treasury.

With or without government help, in total, between 4 January and 13 April 1847, thirty-nine works were recorded for the Barony of Mohill. As well as the large enterprises like the Canal and Drainage Scheme, the works also included smaller projects like making a footpath in Mohill town at a cost of

£150 and building a new road from Stuck to Corrabeagh at £1,900. Other works included finishing and completing the road from Rooskey to Mohill, making a new road between Gort and Drumdoo, and repairing "451 perches of road between the road newly made from Gortletteragh Chapel to Drumhirk River at Cloone".

While these local relief and public works helped, they were just not enough to stave off the effects of the famine. On road projects, men could earn two pence a day while women could expect a penny for a day's work hauling clay and stones. Food would be included—a bowl of porridge before starting in the morning and another on finishing in the evening. Where food was not included, wages could go up to four pence a day. This was far too little to feed most large families, especially once the price of corn increased. The Inspecting officer for public and relief works in Leitrim reported that "the miserable condition of the half-famished people is greatly increased by the exorbitant . . . price of meal and provisions, in so much that the wages gained by them on the works are quite inadequate to purchase a sufficiency to feed many large families". Often too, the neediest families were too weak to participate and were left helpless.

By the end of 1846, the numbers of starving soared. As if lack of food wasn't enough, the winter of 1846 was long and harsh with snow falling up until April the following year. In the unrelenting cold and damp, thousands died from dysentery, cholera and other diseases. More perished on the public works programmes, some collapsing from sheer exhaustion. Relief works themselves were frequently halted by passing funerals. Local newspapers in Carrick-on-Shannon and Mohill told harrowing tales of old women walking the road to the cemetery to die and of whole families being buried where they died, in their small mud cabins or by the side of the road. Bishop O'Higgins of Ardagh in a letter to Paul Cullen, rector of the Irish College in Rome, wrote that "711 died during last season in Gortleitra—one of our ordinary county parishes—Most of them were buried by night in bags, cabbage plots, and in the cabins where they departed". If families were lucky, their dead were hauled to a mass grave for burial (in Mohill, this was in Hyde Street, near the Workhouse). The survivors scratched for food, eating grasses and weeds and wild birds to stay alive. Such was their desperation that some of the starving would go to terrible lengths to get food. In Cloone, one man tried to get through the crush for a cup of Indian meal: he climbed over the backs of those in front of him, but fell into the boiler and died from the resulting burns. Another woman attacked and pulled the tongue out of a dog to get at a stack of potatoes that the dog was guarding.

Soup kitchens

In the face of continuing crisis, the government continued to demonstrate its short-termist approach. In the spring of 1847, it decided that the public works had failed to save lives and cost too much. Over £5 million had been spent across the country while the thirty-nine works in Mohill had been completed at a cost of £15,368.

The works were to be replaced with soup kitchens distributing cooked food. The works stopped almost immediately leaving incomplete roads and half-finished projects. Men and women who had struggled to maintain their families on the wages they earned on works now found themselves unemployed and penniless. While they waited for the soup kitchens to be set up, some turned in desperation to crime. Thefts of food and animals increased dramatically and bailiffs and rent collectors reported increasing incidences of violence as they went about trying to collect rent and rates. Such was the level of disturbance in Mohill that it was one of the areas covered by a new ban on the carrying of unlicensed arms.

The soup kitchens, when they were finally set up were effective but short-lived. At their peak, they were feeding over three-million people a day throughout Ireland. In Mohill, the government-supplied 60-gallon pot was used to feed up to three hundred people a day and a small bakery was set up to provide bread. In Cloone, the wife of the Church of Ireland Minister, Mrs Hogg oversaw the distribution of soup to four hundred people a week. In Leitrim the soup came with no conditions; in other counties the price of taking the soup was high: it required the taker to convert to Protestantism. One of the reasons for the short life of the soup kitchens was the over-enthusiastic proselytising on the part of some Protestant administrators in places like Mayo, Galway and Roscommon where 'taking the soup' meant a chance of life but with a new religion.

As the famine showed little signs of abating, the government became determined to put responsibility for financing of famine relief squarely in the hands of Irish taxpayers. After only a few months of operation, the soup kitchens were wound up.

Religion and relief

While the government and local officials lurched from initiative to initiative or argued about the degree to which the famine even existed, it was left largely to voluntary and religious groups to alleviate the suffering.

Amongst all these groups, the Society of Friends, or Quakers, provided the most continuous and practical supply of relief through the worst of the famine years. Their relief effort was organised, targeted and channelled through one or two carefully vetted people in each local area. The Quaker records show a continuous flow of money, food and clothing to people like the local Church of Ireland minister, Arthur Hyde[23], as well as WH Foster and Letitia Veevers in Mohill. They received regular sums of ten to thirty pounds, clothing grants and deliveries of one or two tons of Indian meal and rice which they distributed as they saw fit. In Cloone, the Rev. Andrew Hogg and his wife were acknowledged to have done sterling work on behalf of the starving.

Joseph Bewley, one of the joint secretaries of the Society of Friends Committee, pointed out that "there were none were more efficient than the Protestant Clergy", made more efficient because "they had the great benefit of having the aid

---

[23] Arthur Hyde spent fifty-four years in Mohill, from 1816-1870. (Arthur's grandson, Douglas Hyde, founded the Gaelic League in 1893 who was elected President of Ireland in 1938.)

of their wives and daughters in attending to the poor". The Catholic clergy, while being "exceedingly useful", did not, he noted, have the advantage of help from wives and daughters.

Of the direct role played by the local Catholic clergy, we know little. The Catholic parish priest at Mohill was John William Eivers who was in the post for forty-two years from 1839-1881. Because of the length of his tenure, and the fact that he went on to be Canon and Dean, it would be fair to surmise that he would have had far more in common with the wealthier sections of his community than with the poor; he was also known to be successful in getting rid of curates who might take an anti-landlord stance.[24] Overall, the Catholic clergy tended to focus on their role as priests, bringing last rites and instruction to the dying. A number of priests described being besieged by the sick and dying who cried at their door for help. John Madden, parish priest in the neighbouring county of Roscommon, wrote in desperation. "My house is surrounded by them . . . calling for Work or Food . . . We are doing what we can to distribute Soup. What can we do? The Applicants are so numerous; our means so limited". Another priest, Hugh Quigley, wrote about his long day, from four in the morning until five in the evening holding Confession and administering "consolation and instruction" "for the convenience of the poor country people, who . . . flock in thousands . . . to prepare themselves for the death they look to as inevitable". After a full day, he

---

[24] Dean Eivers did, however, leave ten guineas in his will to be paid annually at Christmas to the poor of Newtownforbes.

would arrive home to sit down to his dinner, but found it interrupted by the "groans and sobs" of people crying at his door. "In truth the Priest must either harden his heart against the cry of misery, or deprive himself of his usual nourishment to keep victims from falling at his door". The Catholic Church was more successful in fund-raising through its wide network overseas and especially through the Irish College in Rome. Pope Pius IX sent 1,000 Roman dollars to the Irish bishops in January 1847 and in March called on the Catholic Church worldwide to provide prayers and money. The Church in France, Italy, Belgium, the Netherlands, the German states, Austria and other European countries all contributed money for relief.

Other appeals are launched across the world. The very first donation to the Irish Famine was raised in India at the end of 1845 by British troops serving in Calcutta. A further appeal to British people living in India raised almost £14,000. Contributions were received from the Tsar of Russia, the Sultan of the Ottoman Empire and from the government of Barbados. Money also came from Australia, South Africa, Mexico, Tobago, Antigua and the Seychelles. In England, a group calling itself 'The British Association for the Relief of Extreme Distress in Ireland and Scotland' was founded by Stephen Spring Rice, Lionel de Rothschild and Thomas Baring. It was successful in raising large sums of money from the wealthy classes of English society. Queen Victoria gave £2,000 and proclaimed a day of fast and prayer. (She also visited Ireland in 1949, though she received little welcome from the general population who blamed her and her government for their plight.) People in the United States were the most generous. Contributions were recorded from State governments, mayors, soldiers, bishops, priests, the Jewish community and Choctaw Indians of present-day Oklahoma[25]. The Society of Friends in New York recognised that their ability to work so effectively in Ireland was due in large part to "the munificent bounty of the citizens of the United States". Most generous of all were the Irish emigrants who were "silently drafting their little savings to their relatives at home": their total contribution would amount to millions of dollars over the course of the Famine.

Mohill Board of Guardians

When the government decided to hand responsibility for famine relief to the local Board of Guardians, it was effectively asking them to fund all famine relief out of the rates they raised, i.e. out of their own pockets. But even if they had been willing, they would be able to do little without a significant increase in poor rates. The rates on Lough Rynn were about £15: they would hardly have made a dent in the £15,000 the works in Mohill had cost in the previous two years.

Poor rates for the area in 1847 were set as follows:

Mohill	£- . 3 . 6½
Annaduff	£- . 2 . 11
Ballinamore	£- . - . 10

[25] The Choctaw Indians donated $710 just 16 years after their own 'trail of tears'—a forced re-settlement march during which one quarter of the migrating population died.

Cloone	£- . 2 . 3½
Eslin	£- . 1 . 10½
Newtowngore	£- . - . 10
Rynn	£- . 3 . 1½
Aughavas	£- . 2 . 8½
Annaghveagh	£- . 2 . 8½
Carrigallen	£- . 2 . 11
Drumreilly	£- . 4 . 2
Fenagh	£- . 1 . 0½
Oughteragh	£- . 2 . 1

Fig. 22: Poor Rate for the Electoral Divisions of Mohill, 1847

With two further legislative acts, the government washed its hands of the problem in Ireland. In 1847, it declared the famine to be over and imposed a restriction on whatever relief was still available. A new Clause sponsored by Sir William Gregory of Coole Park in Galway barred all but the most destitute from receiving relief. Those with holdings valued at more than £6, i.e. more than a quarter of an acre, would no longer be entitled to receive help. However, in practice, the ban proved largely inoperable.

The famine, of course, was far from over in 1847. There was some cause for optimism and there did seem to be a reduction in those requesting help: by the beginning of September 1847, the number of inmates in Mohill Workhouse had dropped to 465 from a consistent high of over 700 through the previous eighteen months. However, although there was little blight in 1847, the crop was small and neither the land nor the people had recovered from the pervasive disease and hunger. In addition, many smallholders had been unable to pay rent during the previous two years and were now facing large bills for arrears, and an increasing threat of eviction.

Although tenants at Rynn were to face eviction later for non-payment of rent during the famine, there is in fact no evidence that tenants were evicted en masse during the famine years.

While the previous two years had been hugely difficult, the real hardship was in fact only beginning. In 1847, the number of people admitted to Mohill workhouse soared to 1,275. By February 1850, it held 1,810—more than double its capacity.

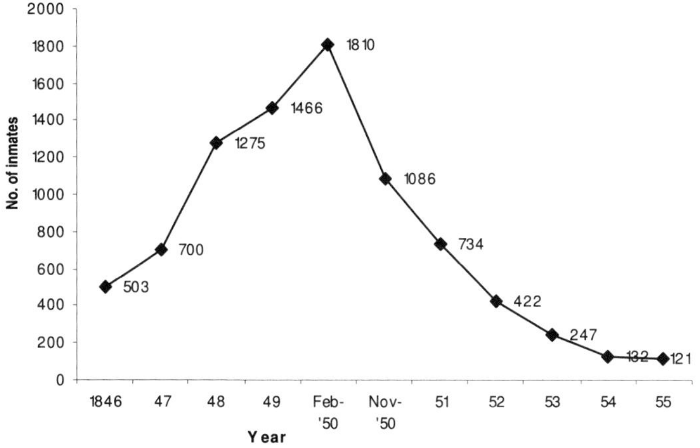

Fig. 23: Inmates in Mohill Workhouse, 1846–1855

Even in good times, the workhouse was an undesirable option for the destitute: families were forcibly split up, living conditions were bad and food was inadequate. In the bad years of the famine, it was the last resort of the hopeless. When the workhouse opened in 1842, adult inmates could expect a breakfast of seven ounces of oatmeal with a half-pint of milk and for dinner, three-and-a-half pounds of potatoes with a pint of buttermilk.

By 1847, the potatoes and milk were gone and adults were limited to a dinner of eight ounces of oatmeal. At one meeting of the Board of Guardians, it was agreed that rice would be added to the dinner on three days a week and meat would be offered as a treat on Christmas Day. There is reason to believe that even these meagre rations were not dispensed and that the money supplied to pay for them disappeared into the pockets of the workhouse managers.

By April 1847, having reached the capacity it was designed for, the Board of Guardians concluded that it was not "expedient to admit any more applicants on account of the Sickness prevailing in the House, the want of proper officers and the confusion of the accounts". They also resolved that, considering the Union's heavy level of debt, the dead would, in future, be interred without a coffin. They argued that the feelings of a dead person's loved ones could hardly be "more hurt than they are at present", given the "melancholy and distressing state of destitution and hopelessness in which they have been thrown".

By summer, the situation in Mohill was such that it was listed as one of twenty-two officially "distressed" Unions[26].

[26] The 'distressed' Unions formed a nearly continuous line down the whole of the west coast from Glenties in Donegal to south Kerry, and inland from Galway to Leitrim.

As the famine increased its grip, it became obvious that the management of Mohill workhouse was incompetent in its response to the crisis. Clements was one of many who complained about the Mohill Board. Although the complaints were taken to government level, they were dismissed as having no real substance and attributed to Clements's personal animosity to the Poor Law and its administrators. While it is true that Clements did irritate the administration in Dublin Castle with needless submissions, his animosity came from a genuine belief that the government's incompetence had caused the Famine. In this case, Clements' irritation was justified. In short, the Mohill Board of Guardians was apathetic and uninterested in organising themselves to deal with the growing crisis. This general attitude could be a cause of or a result of a very high turnover of workhouse management and staff during the period. Four Board members resigned. Some members of staff were lost to death or illness, but in one case the Master and Matron were sacked because the Board disapproved of their marriage. In another, the workhouse clerk, John Clarke who looked after the workhouse accounts was sacked from his position when the Commissioners deemed him "unfit for office". (A month later he was to be found holding the same position in Carrick workhouse.) There were also continued reverberations from the prosecution of three Board members in January 1846. By late 1847, Mohill Union was drowning in debt and contractors were refusing to supply the workhouse. The Poor Law Commissioners had enough evidence to justify removing the Board and replacing it with salaried

'Vice-Guardians'. Probably in anticipation of opposition, they picked a time when Lord Clements was away from home.

The Vice-Guardian's submitted their report to the Poor Law Commissioners within a week: in it, they condemned the management of Mohill workhouse and painted a vivid picture of the place as a filthy, lawless, neglected pit whose funds were probably siphoned off by members of the Board of Guardians:

> "The building we found most dilapidated, and fast advancing to ruin, everything out of repair, the yards undrained and filled, in common with the cesspools, by accumulations of filth—a violation of all sanitary requirements; fever and dysentery prevailing throughout the house, every ward filthy to a most noisome degree, evolving offensive effluvia; the paupers defectively clothed, and many of those recently admitted continuing in their own rags and impurity; classification and separation set at nought; a general absence of utensils and implement; the dietary not adhered to, and the food given in a half-cooked state—most inadequate, particularly for the sick; the meals distributed through the medium of one-sixth the number of vessels required, and uproar and confusion, the stronger securing an over quantity to the privation of the weaker, and the breakfast not completely dispensed until late in the evening; no contracts existing, no stores of provisions to meet even the wants of a day; the able-bodied not employed, and without restraint or discipline; the

> destruction of all description of Union property proceeding rapidly, many hundreds' pounds worth appearing to be missing; the children in the schools receiving no education or industrial training, in other respects their neglected state painfully exhibited by their diseased and emaciated aspect; no means for the proper treatment of the sick, the officers ignorant of their duties; coffins unused in the internment of the dead."

Fig. 24: Report on Mohill Workhouse, 1847

The Vice-Guardian's task was not an easy one. Over the next few months, they complained frequently about the interminable difficulties they faced: the "useless" workhouse officers and a "most worthless set" of workmen ensured that repairs were made slowly and with reluctance. They were also frustrated by their inability to find anyone to take on the job of Poor Rate collector. Despite being offered the "extravagant rate of fees (two shillings in the pound)", "proper persons" were, apparently, deterred from taking the job by a host of issues, including:

> "The extreme poverty of the area, which we regret to say, is retrograding still further every day, every description of chattel property fast disappearing its lawless state, the unusually high rates, and the previous irregular habits formed in meeting this species of demand."

By December 1847, the positions of the Poor Law Union in the whole country were in such a state of chaos that the administration suspended the functions of all the local voluntary Boards of Guardians and replaced them with salaried administrators. Unfortunately, many of these drew the salary but did little.

Emigration

As the famine progressed, emigration was seen as the best option for many who found their way to the workhouse. The new Board made money available to buy suits of clothes for inmates whose (mostly female) relatives had sent home money to pay their passage to America or Van Diemen's Land (Tasmania). In some cases, funds were provided to contribute to the cost of passage. Between 1845-'55, nearly two million people emigrated from Ireland to America and Australia, and another 750,000 to Britain, the largest single population movement of the 19th century. Thousands died on board 'coffin ships' as they crossed the Atlantic to America. Thousands more died soon after they arrived.

In 1848, Mohill Workhouse responded to a request from the Colonial Lands & Emigration Commissioners in London for female migrants to Australia. Women and girls were wanted as workers and wives to balance out the disproportionately male population that had grown in Australia out of the high rates of transportation. The girls in Mohill were typical: aged 15 to 18, the girls were not orphans, but were selected by the master, matron and chaplain for their good health and moral character. And they were supported by the girls' parents who saw emigration as the only chance of freedom for their children. The girls were sent on their way with a box of supplies, including petticoats, gowns, shoes, a shawl and bonnet, two pounds of soap and a prayer book. At least forty-five girls are known to have been shipped from Mohill: two separate groups landed in Sydney, Australia, one in 1848, the other in 1850.

A changed estate

From all the evidence available, Viscount Clements and his family did as much as any of their peers, and more than most, to alleviate suffering during the famine. Unlike many, Clements could not be accused of being an 'absentee' landlord. The Earl of Leitrim, alongside all of the landed classes, saw huge reductions in his rental income for these years and many of the ascendancy were ruined: one in ten was bankrupted. As the famine progressed, the 2nd Earl grew increasingly fearful of the effects of the famine on his estate and legacy. His concerns about the cost of relief and the growing arrears on his estate are noted in successive codicils to his will where he reduced the annuities and lump sums left to his wife, daughters and others.

In 1849 the harvest was reasonably good and the Famine was declared officially over. Of course it wasn't, but the adequate harvest provided enough of an excuse for the government to hand the Union affairs back to the local Board of Guardians. While Clements may have complained about the Mohill Board in the past, it was nothing to his horror at the state in which the Union was returned. The cost of the relief efforts and the running of the workhouse had created huge debt. The reinstated Board was expected, through local poor rates, to meet an overdraft of nearly £6,000 and continue to deliver solace to the 2,500 people still seeking relief. The Board, and especially Lord Clements, were livid. Clements wrote to the

Commissioners expressing his fury with the decision and describing it as "a most unbounded, arbitrary and despotic exercise of the power of the Poor Law Commissioners."

He recommended that the Board should not re-take control of the Union's affairs, since it had been "handed back in such a disreputable manner". The Board petitioned the Lord Lieutenant to receive a deputation to hear their grievances. The letter was strongly and concisely worded and signed by Clements as Chairman. He received a curt reply from the Lord Lieutenant's Under-Secretary rejecting the plea. Clements wrote back an angry, bitter letter in which he expressed his "deepest distrust" of the Poor Law Commissioners. In January 1850, he further wrote:

> "While we have been given the semblance of free institutions, we live, in point of fact, under a despotism which neither respects the rights of industry or of property engaged in the cultivation of the land. With an unjust law so administered, it is vain and hopeless to expect prosperity or happiness."

The letter, it appears, went unanswered. In fury, Clements had the entire correspondence copied and sent to the newspapers. He continued for years to publish contentious correspondence between him and the administration, and did so with such frequency and impact that it became known as 'Leitrimising'.

After the famine

The Great Famine decimated the population through a combination of disease, starvation and emigration. In the early 1840s Ireland's population was 8,200,000. During the famine years of 1845–51, Ireland lost some 2,225,000 people. Leitrim was as bad, if not worse, than anywhere: the 'excess mortality' rate here was amongst the highest in the country. At 42.9 per 1000, it was exceeded only by Galway, Roscommon, Cavan, Sligo and Mayo. Between 1841–'61, Leitrim lost a third of its population, decreasing from over 150,000 to 104,000; 28% had been lost in the ten years from 1851 to '61. (The decline continued until well the beginning of this century and today numbers 29,000.) In those twenty years of loss, not only were the numbers significant, but also the type of people that were most effected.

While the details of those suffering are harrowing, the actual numbers who received relief by no means encompassed the whole population. In Mohill, for example, the most people receiving relief at any time represented one seventh of the total population, and while this might well not cover all of those who needed relief, it is still indicative. Most farmers, merchants and mid-sized landholders survived the Famine and indeed many benefited from it.

It was the labourers and their families who had, by far, suffered the greatest effects of the famine. Between 1841 and 1851, 83% of the poorest houses were destroyed or left empty; at the same time, the number of large farmhouses doubled. At the same time, the chief source of employment and income shifted: the numbers engaged in the 'Direction of Labour' (i.e. farmers and merchants) doubled, while the numbers depending on their 'Own manual labour' were slashed to a quarter of the 1841 figure.

The whole labouring class effectively disappeared.

Census of County Leitrim 1841–1861

		Males				
Year	Area in statute acres	Heads of family & children	Visitors	Servants	Total males	Total males and females
1841	393,363	66,830	7,274	3,397	77,501	155,397
1851	392,363	49,090	5,411	3,610	56,111	111,897
1861	376,212	46,591	3,715	2,256	52,562	104,744
		Females				
Year	Area in statute acres	Heads of family & children	Visitors	Servants	Total females	Total males and females
1841	393,363	63,021	10,065	3,910	77,796	155,397
1851	392,363	46,078	6,578	3,130	55,786	111,897
1861	376,212	44,874	4,339	2,469	52,182	104,744

Fig. 25: Census figures for County Leitrim

Employment

	Families classified according to their:			
	Pursuits as chiefly employed in:			
Year	Agriculture	Trades, Manuf'ng, etc	Other pursuits	
1841	21,663	4,067	1,461	
1851	14,680	2,702	2,815	
1861	12,483	1,881	5,177	
	Families classified according to their:			
	Means as chiefly dependent on:			
Year	Vested means, Professions, etc	The direction of labour	Their own manual labour	Means not specified
1841	508	5,799	20,479	406
1851	879	11,277	7,068	975
1861	1,016	12,024	4,957	1,544

Fig. 26: Employment in County Leitrim (1)

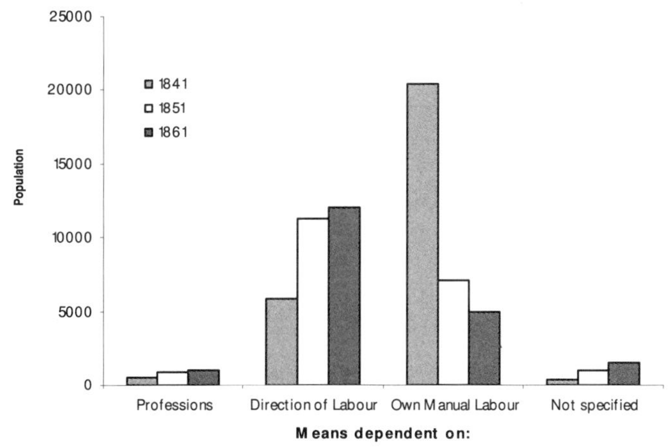

Fig. 27: Employment in County Leitrim (2)

Housing*

Year	Area in statute acres	Total number of houses	Average number per house
1841	393,363	26,649	6
1851	392,363	19,753	6
1861	376,212	19,284	5.5

Year	Inhabited houses				
	Class 1	Class 2	Class 3	Class 4	Total inhabited
1841	152	3,221	11,340	11,119	25,912
1851	225	4,319	11,358	3,011	18,913
1861	301	5,801	10,696	1,893	18,691

Fig. 28: Housing in Leitrim by year and class of house (1)

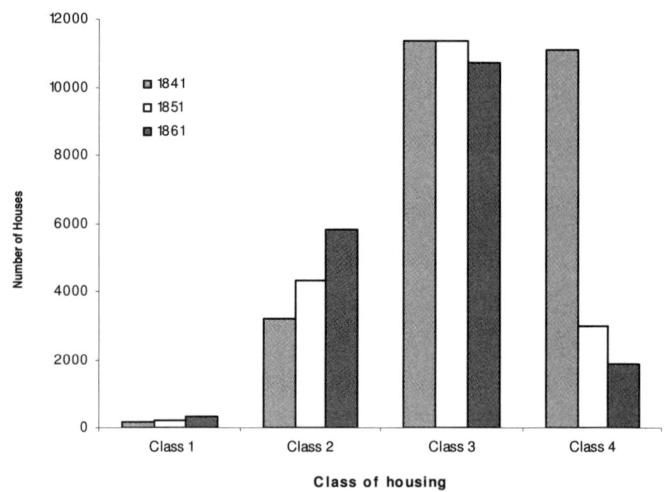

Fig. 29: Housing in Leitrim by year and class of house (2)

**Class 1: homes of large farmers, estate managers, and professional classes;*
Class 2: good farm houses or town houses, maybe over two stories;
Class 3: thatched cottages, two to four rooms with windows;
Class 4:12 foot square, one-roomed, windowless mud cabins that were home to the poor labouring class.

Fig. 30: A cottage outside Mohill, 1889

Taken by Leland Duncan Lewis and reprrinted with permission.

For the majority of survivors, the solution was emigration. Of those who emigrated from Ireland between 1851-55, it is estimated that 80-90% were farm labourers or servants, i.e. Catholic, Irish-speaking[27] and illiterate. Leitrim had one of the highest emigration rates of all. As the population small landholdings were frequently subsumed into larger ones. If they had not died or emigrated during the Famine, the labourers and smallholders were now faced with the threat of sweeping land-clearance. And amongst the old and new landholders, there was little sense of loss. Indeed it was referred to by one Northern Whig politician as "the present favourable crisis". When William Gregory was putting through his Gregory Clause, it was suggested that the provision would destroy the small farmers: he replied that he "could not see of what use such small farmers could possibly be". Lord Palmerston, Foreign Secretary and an Irish landlord, spoke for more than a few when he postulated: "Any great improvement in the social system in Ireland must be founded upon an extensive change in the present state of agrarian occupation, and that this change necessarily implies a long, continued and systematic rejectment of small holders and of squatting cottiers". And many of this landed class, as evangelical Protestants, felt that the Famine was no less than God's own solution to eradicate 'popery', 'priestcraft' and all that went with it. William Carleton was not the only one who

[27] In 1851, the figure for Irish speakers in Leitrim was the lowest in Connaught and lower than the country average: 0.13% of the population spoke Irish only; 13.28% spoke Irish and English.

explained the famine thus: "we feel that the people must die off … This is a blessed famine, God be praised".

However abhorrent as policy, the economic impact of the Famine meant greater prosperity and sustained development for those who remained. Small plots were subsumed into more economic land-holdings. And for those few of the labouring class who remained, there was little work as agriculture moved away from arable-based agriculture to less labour-intensive livestock farming.

A transformed land

Just five years after the worst of the Famine, the area around Lough Rynn and Mohill had recovered remarkably.

According to Slater's Directory of 1856, Mohill was a prosperous, thriving market town whose principal trade was in "corn, provisions and yarn".

> "(Main Street) contains several good shops well-stocked with the various articles of fashion and of local requisites. Great progress is manifest in its general appearance and of its size is considered one of the most stirring, and is certainly the most thriving town of any in the surrounding counties."

The town had three hotels and posting houses and five public houses. The main street was lined with shops including apothecaries, boot & shoe makers, haberdashers, a baker, nail-maker, saddler, feather dealer, dyer, tailor, five drapers and as many as nine 'general dealers'. Further progress was planned with the completion of the Dublin-Sligo railroad in 1862.

There were also regular social events like the Mohill Races, held in May each year. While some of these holidays were marred by fights, others were peaceful events when the extra police brought in for the day could join in the festivities. And they drew large crowds. The first race of the annual races, the Mohill Traders' Plate carried a prize of 30 sovereigns and would attract a "vast concourse of people" spread out across the hills of Boeshill and Coolabawn. From these vantage points, the spectators had a perfect view of the racecourse below and of the surrounding countryside stretching as far as Lough Rynn. A contemporary reporter writes of his contentment contemplating a view that was "a prospect seldom to be seen in other parts of Ireland yet quite unknown and less appreciated".

For those who survived or chose to remain in Ireland after the Famine, the social map of the country had changed for ever. And the recovery was sustained right through to the present time: never again would Ireland experience the insidious cycle of famine that characterised earlier decades and centuries. Many of the old values and traditions were lost, and English mores were adopted. Irish ceased to be used at all: it was discouraged by English-speaking teachers and parents who believed their children had a more promising future if they spoke English.

Men and women waited longer to marry and more people remained single. And the land became the focus of attention. Farmers' daughters could offer substantial dowries and marriages were calculatedly arranged around the land and its potential for economic gain. (This all helped to give Irish wives a higher economic status than in most other rural societies). Illegitimacy rates also decreased, due less to the Church's influence and more to obligations to family and kin. Education was important, with high levels of literacy, and attendance at school was encouraged—though you were twice as likely to be able to read and write if you were a boy. By 1861, two-thirds of men over the age of fifteen could at least read, and nearly half could read and write. (This compared well with progressive European countries and was significantly better than the countries in the east and south of Europe.)

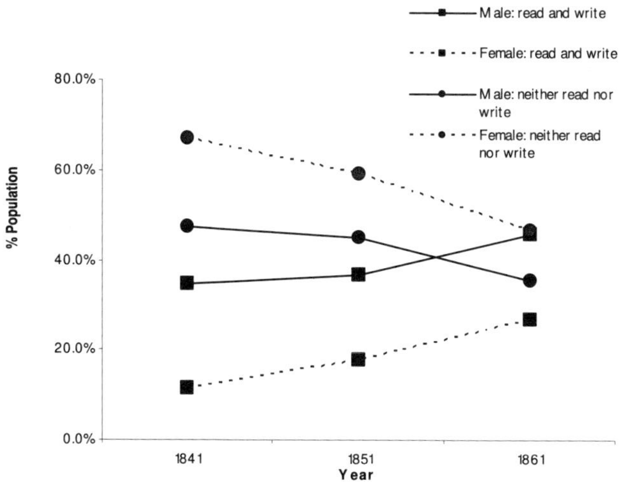

Fig. 31: Literacy in County Leitrim (1)

Census of County Leitrim 1841–1861: Literacy

	Education (persons aged 15 years and upwards)							
	Who can read and write		Who can read only		Who can neither read nor write			
Year	M	F	M	F	M	F	Total males	Total females
1841	23,208	7,773	11,995	14,318	31,664	45,165	66,867	67,256
1851	18,460	8,940	9,225	11,395	22,537	29,558	50,222	49,893
1861	20,578	12,044	8,498	12,014	16,109	20,972	45,185	45,030

Fig. 32: Literacy in County Leitrim (2)

Newspapers were widely read, and they were by no means limited to local stories. Reports covered a range of topics and were carried on places as far away as Egypt and Abyssinia, India, the United States, Britain and the rest of Ireland. Advertisements from London-based watchmakers and wine-sellers ran alongside those for local services and products.

While the world had changed utterly for the underclasses, the emerging middle-classes were able to support a growing and prosperous economy. (Ireland was the seventh richest country in the world in 1870.) Their homes were more comfortable, and they could increasingly afford to spend money on furnishings and decoration, maybe buying a new deal table or a dresser for the kitchen or fancy curtains for the parlour. And they didn't have to go far to spend their money: Mohill had everything they could need.

Slater's 1881 Directory shows just how much development happened in the twenty-five years from Lewis' 1856 report. Slater lists some sixty-seven different businesses in the town of Mohill, including: eleven bakers (up from two in 1846); two new banks; four boot and shoe makers; two butchers;

four carpenters and cart-makers; three 'china, glass and earthenware dealers'; two coopers; twenty-one grocers; six hardwaremen; eight linen and woollen drapers and haberdashers; seven milliners and dressmakers; two nail-makers; two seed and guano dealers; twenty-three 'spirit and porter retailers'; two tailors; four timber and iron merchants. Public transport was available to Dromod railway station every morning at ten past eleven.

Coercion, crime and sectarian convulsions

Throughout the period of the Famine and the years immediately after, the undercurrent of tension and unrest continued and occasionally erupted into violent disturbances. Prior to and during the famine, Leitrim was one of the most 'disturbed' counties in Ireland. The situation was so bad in Mohill that it was one of the areas covered by the Prevention of Crime and Outrage in Ireland Bill passed at the end of 1847. The Bill dealt with the immediate perceived threat of crime and violence by prohibiting the carrying and holding of unlicensed arms.

As the country recovered from the Famine, the grievances continued, mostly between the dispossessed labourers and their farmer landlords, and between larger landholders and the new tenants, the emerging small farming class. Such was the level of grievance in Leitrim that it was one of the few counties to produce "intense sectarian convulsions" in 1852.

Over time, the tenants' resentments began to be accompanied by a growing sense of nationalism and political power. In 1850, the vote had been extended to tenants with holdings valued at more than £12: in the 1850s and '60s this covered about 12 acres (rents had increased in line with prices). In the 1852 election in Leitrim, the constituency that had consistently voted the Liberal Clements' as M.P., returned a Tory and a Radical for the first time. (Though Mohill electoral division continued its support for the liberals, giving the Tory candidate only 9% of its vote.)

The tenants' growing political awareness would culminate later in the Land League and Home Rule movements, but in the 1850s and '60s was manifesting itself in resentment and isolated acts of rebellion and the increasing prevalence of organised insurgent 'Secret Societies'.

Through the 1850s, farmers and labourers were the main protagonists and victims of crime as they become locked in a conflict over occupation of land, rent, unemployment and labourers' wages. Farmers were the target for over sixty per cent of all crime and for twenty-seven percent of homicides. "Labourers and servants" accounted for thirty-nine per cent of homicides, and "gentlemen and agents", eight per cent.

Much of the crime was organised through the Secret Societies and the courts could not rely on victims helping them get a conviction. Even though the victims frequently knew the perpetrators, they tended not to co-operate with the police or courts and there was general suspicion of any actions by the magistrates or police.

In 1851, there was a fire in Lough Rynn Castle, but the local Royal Irish Constabulary managed to extinguish it before it could cause much damage. Clements championed a Head

Constable, McManus, who was demoted and transferred for over-zealous action in putting out a fire without informing his superior officer. It is not known what caused the fire, but at that time the Molly Maguires[28] were quite active around Cloone and it could well have been an act of arson.

Clements's father, the 2nd Earl, attacked the authorities for allowing the people's misery to become so extreme that they were reduced to desperation and lawlessness. He blames the government squarely for the "neglect and bad laws" that, he said, were directly responsible for the wave of agrarian outrage that was being experienced that year. He wrote:

> "Why does such a state of things exist? Such things do not exist when the people are prosperous and contented. . . Midnight outrages of the kind in question always originate in the misery of the people. When heavy burdens are laid upon them; when social tyranny oppresses them; when hunger stares them in the face or tugs at their hearts—then they become desperate. And when their social superiors neglect and the law ignores a people, is it a matter of wonder that they become desperate? . . The extreme of misery . . . renders (some) recklessly active. . . . In Leitrim it has produced this.

---

[28] The 'Molly Maguires' was one of many 'Secret Societies' or 'Ribbon Societies' that emerged around 1843: it was a vigilante-type secret organisation that fought for tenant rights. Much of the politically-derived crime in the 1850s was attributed to them.

> Leitrim is a proverbially miserable and neglected county. The land is neglected; the people are permitted to grow and wither and rot—a field of breathing weeds; those to whom providence, or law, has given the property of the county seem to have no sense of responsibility.
>
> People cannot be expected to cultivate a good behaviour when they are baptised in wretchedness. They ought certainly to obey the law: but they will ask "what has the law done for us?" and that no man can answer. Let them have the means of life—let them get out of pig-stys and rags—let them have food fit for human beings—give them encouragement to toil—bestow hope upon them (a thing they know nothing of) and we will answer for the good conduct of the Leitrim people.
>
> Let it be borne in mind, as an axiom in Social Economy, that social outrages are committed only by a miserable people; and that a miserable people are made by neglect and bad laws."

As the land clearances gained pace, evictions were frequent and those who took over the homes and lands of evicted tenants were often subject to abuse, their new homes burned or wrecked. Some were murdered. In 1851, two threatening letters were found in the house of Obadia Mee in Mohill directing him to "clear out of that country" or to "expect the same death as Brooks", a farmer who had been brutally murdered. The notices also threatened William Lawder, the

Agent and the Bailiff Henry Huston with similar treatment, for "presuming to stock the country with Co. Cavan Protestants". It appeared that a number of those who took over lands of evicted tenants were from Co. Cavan and were "now daily suffering injuries" from their new neighbours.

Labourers were targeted and threatened as a way to get at the landholders. In one instance, workers on their way to Francis Nisbett's farm were warned by a gang, armed and firing shots, not to work for under a shilling a day or to "mark the consequences". These assaults were usually carried out by organised gangs like the Molly Maguires. According to the court there was "a gang of able-bodied robbers committing outrages every night in the town and neighbourhood who carry out their depredations without the least fear of molestation". After two particularly brutal murders, the priest in Mohill pronounced a curse for five years on all those who joined these groups.[29]

As local Justice of the Peace, Clements had his hands full. Apart from the general sense of lawlessness pervading the country-side, Mohill was a fairly lively spot with frequent riots and fights, many of which had no political or sectarian basis. In 1853, in an effort to return the town to some semblance of Christian order, the shops were banned from opening on Sundays. A local shopkeeper called it a "harsh illegal and arbitrary order . . . rendered still more so when

---

[29] It was not uncommon for priests to use the pulpit to impose curses, 'stares' or 'threats of sickness' to direct their parishioners rather than relying on Roman law.

enforced by our tyrannical police officer Mr Waters, whose bad feeling towards the poor people of this country has already been well tested".

Fair day could be hazardous: as well as avoiding one of many fights that erupted, people had to watch out for the "numerous gangs" of petty thieves and pick-pockets that roamed the fair. Constable Crowe had a busy time breaking up the regular fracas. Sometimes the police themselves were the subject of attack. In one case, two constables who tried to break up a riot were assaulted and beaten "in a most savage manner". (It is not recorded whether one of them was the tyrannical Mr. Waters.)

There were varying opinions as to the efficacy of the police in stopping crime: in February 1851, the local newspaper carried a story, of which they were "informed by several parties", that "when some of the force go on patrol at night, they wend their way to houses in the neighbourhood to woo some lovesick maidens who have a *war-like taste!*" (Newspaper's italics.)

Amongst the catalogue of offences recorded in the Petty Sessions in Mohill, there are reports of shots being fired, windows broken and arson attacks on houses; not to mention burglaries, robberies, poisoning, infanticide and cattle-stealing. Mrs. Little's hotel was burgled, and even the Church in Mohill was robbed, the thieves making away with chalices, surplices, pew candles and other items. And individuals did not hesitate to use the law to right injustices. In one session at Mohill, a Maria Cashian won a case against her employer Pat Conefrey who, she claimed, failed to pay her a quarter's wages. In the same session Ann McGarty, four months into her marriage, sued her husband Pat for beating her and making her life miserable. Every week, there were cases of farmers suing each other over cattle and asses trespassing on neighbours' property. Some tenants resorted to entreating Clements to right wrongs perpetrated by their own family. He received one letter from a Mrs McKeon beseeching him to intervene to return land and a cabin to her which her son and daughter-in-law had "cruelly" taken over:

> To the Honourable Lord Viscount Clements
>
> The Humble Memorial of the Widow McKeon of Clooncarne in the parish of Mohill most humbly sheweth that the late demised Honourable Lord Viscount Clements bestowed your Memorialist a House and a Rood of Ground in Clooncarne that her son holds the remainder of the farm formerly held by Memorialist's husband that after this Gift given her by Lord Clements her son John McKeon persuaded her to surrender to him the Cabin and Rood of Ground and that he would support her but contrary to his promises she is now much aggrieved by her son and daughterinlaw your poor Memorialist would rather beg if able than live with him he only has by his Craft persuaded the priest Mr Farrell that he has done every thing to the Comfort of Memorialist in order to wipe off the odium of Cruelty exercised by both himself and his wife Memorialist beseeches your Lordship to have her

> Cabin and Rood of Ground returned to her again and she will give him no further trouble during her life and Memorialist in duty bound will always pray.
>
> (from) Widow McKeon

Sentencing

Seen in a modern context, the magistrates' sentencing policy seems, to say the least, inconsistent and hardly commensurate with the crime. Outlaws accused of taking forcible possession of land usually got a sentence of three months in gaol and assault and riot charges usually merited a fine of about 20 shillings. Though sometimes the offenders got gaol sentences, like John Clyne who found himself serving two weeks in gaol for striking John Hunt with a horse-whip on Fair Day. In contrast, the standard sentence for robbery was ten years transportation, with little discrimination between the seriousness of the crime or the criminal intent. At one court, a woman was convicted for stealing linen and a twelve-year old boy was found guilty of stealing bread and clothes: both got ten years transportation. Concealing a birth (a common enough occurrence) warranted one or two months in gaol.

Other offences were dealt with more pragmatically. When fourteen men were brought into Mohill gaol for drinking during unlicensed hours, the Governor "cut their hair close-crop and gave each a cold shower or bath, twenty-four hours in solitary, and then sent them home".

Fig. 33: Mohill Courthouse 1889

Photograph by Leland Duncan Lewis © Irish Picture Library, Davison & Associates

There is some evidence that Clements and his agent, George West, were not too harsh in their sentencing—at least in the early 1850s. In November 1851, West got a threatening letter from the Molly Maguires directing him forthwith to dispossess Richard Reynolds, Clerk of the Petty Sessions, from a house in Cloone rented to him by West, because Reynolds was "obnoxious" and refused public access to a pump on his land. The note implies that they are treating West kindly by giving him notice of their intentions, since he was always a "parchal (sic) juror". In another, the Earl wrote to West, telling him of two outstanding riot cases in Mohill—one at Burbidge's Public House, the other a fight on the previous Fair Day—and suggesting that he might dispose of them "by a small penalty the parties being all in Gaol".

Incidentally, in 1850, the administration instructed the police to carry out a secret enquiry into the character (and probably the political sympathies) of Justices of the Peace. This drew another angry outburst from Clements on the grounds that this was tampering with the rights of the individual and threatened the set up of a police state.

Another concern for the authorities was the anomalous number of people attending the public Dispensary in Mohill. In October 1867, the Medical Officer urged that there be an Enquiry into why there should be 1,104 people seeking treatment in Mohill—three times the number in Carrigallen. The resulting high cost (over £175 a year) of keeping the Dispensary going was one issue, but the other was a deep suspicion that the good people of Mohill were taking undue advantage of the service.

From benevolent paternalism to autocratic control

As time went on, the general discontent among tenants was exacerbated by resentment against Lord Leitrim's increasingly high-handed, and eventually tyrannical, approach to managing his estates. As David Thomson put it in his book 'Woodbrook', "while many estates were wasting from neglect by absentees, Leitrim's suffered from close patronage". But the tenants were not the only ones on the receiving end of the Earl's autocratic actions. Throughout Thomas Larcom's under-secretaryship, the administration at Dublin Castle found itself engaged in noisy squabbles with Lord Leitrim. In 1856, Larcom, wrote "the County was always troublesome, but by far the most troublesome and turbulent thing in it was the noble Earl of that name". And whether it was the local tax collector or the Traffic Manager on the railway, none escaped altercation and argument in their dealings. A series of letters from Lord Leitrim's clerk, William Rose record the visits and responses of the estate to "Huston, the Collector" who had arrived at Lough Rynn to collect Income Tax of £9.18.1½ and Poor Rates of £15.5.10. The first demand was questioned, refuted and ignored at varying levels by Lord Leitrim for a number of weeks, but eventually he capitulated and a cheque covering the original amounts was duly handed over.

It seems that the inheritance of the earldom in 1854 marked a turning point in the way Clements played his role as landlord. On his father's death, Clements gained control over lands in Leitrim, Donegal, Kildare and Galway, covering a total of 94,535 acres (147.7 square miles) and valued at £19,692—

making it one of the largest land-holdings in Ireland. It's effect seems to have been to increase his sense of omnipotence. After gaining the Earldom, Clements's earlier, benevolent paternalism completely disappeared and was replaced with a controlling, despotic approach to dealing with his tenants—and others.

As late as 1954, Shane Leslie felt able and justified in writing a negative and downright vitriolic account of Lord Leitrim in an introduction to his play *Lord Mulroy's Ghost.* The play, he claims, dramatises the life and well-deserved death of Lord Leitrim, a man who "lived on in the midst of his great properties, a terror to man and an offence to God from the year 1854". He repeats and embellishes many of the negative stories and legends surrounding the Earl—including ritual and regular despoiling of virgins on the estates.

In 1858, a ballad emerged in Dublin, telling of the fiendish Earl and the serfdom in which he held his tenants and compares him to his "honoured father":

Some who knew the honoured father
Of this fiend – whom widows curse –
Think a witch in stormy weather
Changed him when he was at nurse.
Born alas! In luckless hour
For his tenants one and all
Who must bend beneath his power
And as serf he held in thrall
But a voice from heaven calling,
Soon the words to him may say
To his frightened soul appalling –
Come to judgement, come away.
Should he be before tomorrow

Numbered with the silent dead
O'er his bier no tear of sorrow
By his tenants would be shed.

There is no doubt that Lord Leitrim committed misdemeanours against his tenants, but whether it would be "charitable to think he was not human at all" as Leslie asserts, is questionable. Quotes from personal diaries of friends of the Earl show he was held in some esteem by at least a few people. John Ynr Burges had married Lord Leitrim's sister and one of the few to hold the Earl in some regard. On the day of Lord Leitrim's assassination, he wrote

> "He, poor, dear fellow, was always a kind and affectionate friend to my daughter Mary. This dreadful end after a long life of trouble and effort to preserve his property is most mysterious. He devoted himself to its improvement and welfare and did all in his human power to benefit as well as to alleviate the sufferings of the poor. The improvements during his time are quite wonderful. The gardens at Lough Rynn showed his taste, and the whole place, from a wilderness, he has left a fine possession".

The truth, as ever, lies somewhere between the two perspectives.

The records of the weekly meetings of the Board of Guardians of Mohill Workhouse also illustrate Lord Leitrim's irascibility. He seems to have enjoyed provoking the board, calling them up on the slightest issue and causing long debates over points of order. He hated late starts to meetings:

when the chairman was two minutes late for successive meetings, he insisted on his agent, Mr West, taking the chair and starting the meeting without the latecomer. During meetings, he had no time for long discussions about points that were perfectly clear to him if not to everyone else. He halted one debate over whether the floor in the workhouse needed urgent work, as had been indicated in a Commissioners' report. As the Board argued one point after another, Lord Leitrim left the meeting and returned moments later declaring that he had just been to the infirmary and that it was "impossible to have a better floor in it; it is a capital floor". Having made his point, he walked out. In another meeting, he argued against an increase in salary for the clerk of the workhouse, interrupting other speakers with frequent points of order. In this case, William Lawder in frustration told him "you are out of order yourself, and you are always so; I will not submit to be interrupted by Lord Leitrim". The Chair, no doubt in fear of retribution from Lord Leitrim, ruled Lawder to be out of order. He was a stickler for rules. In one instance the board wanted the master of the workhouse to join a meeting for a specific discussion. Lord Leitrim argued vociferously against it: in his view only members should attend meetings, no matter how good a contribution an outsider might make. Unusually, he lost this argument. The only other person known to win against Lord Leitrim was 'Big' John Canning, from Carrick-on-Shannon. Canning was appointed to build a new Catholic church, but began work on a different site to the one chosen by Leitrim. When Leitrim happened upon the builders, he ordered them to stop, but Canning carried on mixing mortar. Leitrim physically attacked him, and unusually, Canning retaliated and the two wrestled until the men at the site pulled Canning away. The Earl was frustrated in his ability to avenge the incident since Canning was not one of his tenants. The Earl continued his father's tradition of sponsoring education, but again, he did it his way. He continued to provide clothing for the children—flannel dresses for girls and tweed suits for boys—in return for attending school. In the 1860s, he was still pro-education, but forbade the children to have books at home. His reasons were threefold: the children could not afford books; they had no time at home to study; and if the children studied at home, they would make teachers redundant. His ideas for improvements were often not accepted by the tenants, partly due to an inherent resistance by the tenants, but also because of the Earl's methods of implementing improvements. New ways, such as the introduction of new breeds of cattle and sheep, were forced on tenants rather than through any sort of discussion or diplomacy. And enforcement was thorough: one tenant found all his cattle replaced one morning without any consultation or communication from Lord Leitrim. Neither did the Earl like things being done without his consent. When he found that one tenant had built a new house without seeking his permission, he ordered the roof to be taken off and the chimneys knocked in, though this particular order may have derived more from Lord Leitrim's views on population control. He believed that if he prevented rooms being added to houses, it would have the effect of reducing family size and thereby controlling population growth. He had a habit of supervising work closely. One story tells of a hapless labourer who, as he quietly cut turf, was happened upon by Lord Leitrim who proceeded to instruct him in a more correct and efficient way to handle his implement and then waited and watched while the man continued his work. Another story tells of him directing a Mr. Duignan to re-sow his potatoes because he had not asked for permission to dig them up. When Hugh Murray broke up a "permanent grass field" to sow a crop of potatoes (having been ordered not to do so), Leitrim ordered the man to dig up every seed and to return every sod with the grass uppermost. The Earl also dealt quickly with any recalcitrance from his staff: he sacked his best blacksmith, Jeremiah Johnstone, simply because the man, in contravention of a dictate, allowed tenants on a cold day to warm themselves by his fire while they waited to pay their rent. Those paying their rent were supposed to wait in the yard with their hats off before they were called to the rent-window. And no smoking was allowed. Thomas Boyle, a stable boy at Rynn, recalled in his 'Memories': "If he caught a man smoking at work, he would fine him a shilling—but once he had passed on the smoker usually took up where he had left off, as the Lord was never known to look back. He inspected his workers' houses once a year and if any repairs or painting were needed, he would send tradesmen to effect the repairs immediately. As part of his inspection, he would also examine all the bed linen in the house. If he found that it had been well-repaired but worn, he would have his housekeeper replace it with new linen. But if he found worn linen which the neglectful housewife had made no attempt to repair, he would ignore the woman and walk out of the house leaving her to her worn linen for another year."

Fig. 34: Main Street, Mohill

© *National Library of Ireland, EAS 4036. Reprinted with permission.*

Fig. 35: Station Road, Mohill (the road into Mohill from Lough Rynn)

When reports came to him that the church needed repairs, he paid for it to be done immediately. When a worker was ill, he sent for the doctor to attend him—though this may have been out of concern for missed services than the man's health. The Earl also had ways of dealing with troublesome or disagreeable tenants: if they were lucky, he would pay them to emigrate; else he increased their rents or ordered their eviction. In the town of Mohill, he was frequently seen in the town, doing business or on his way to a meeting of the Board of Guardians. He would ride in through Station Road at a gallop, cracking his whip against his boot and occasionally throwing a handful of gold sovereigns to the peasants who might be by the roadside.

He had an ongoing dispute with the Traffic Manager at the Midland Great Western Railway Company. The rail line had opened in 1862 and the Earl took advantage of this new transport system to move goods between his estates at Killadoon, Co Kildare and Lough Rynn (the rail company had been good enough to build stations convenient to both estates: Maynooth and Dromod). However, the Company seemed incapable of getting goods to Dromod in one piece.

In March 1876, it was an iron bar that was missing. Having received only thirty-four fifteen-foot iron bars instead of the thirty-five ordered, Lord Leitrim was moved to write a pointed letter to the Traffic Manager outlining his expectation to receive "compensation for the loss". When ordering coal later that summer, Lord Leitrim took care to warn the Traffic Manager in advance that he expected the shipment to arrive in its entirety. His agent wrote:

> "His Lordship has ordered twelve tons of coals ... to be sent to the Dromod Station by the Midland Great Western Railway, and His Lordship expects that care shall be taken that the Coal is properly weighed and that no loss shall be sustained in transit".

The Traffic Manager—perhaps knowing he had geographical distance and authority behind him—responded and became one of the few people to win an altercation with the Earl. He vouched for the safe transport of the goods, but added a charge for the extra security. William Rose was forced to write back:

> "I am directed by the Earl of Leitrim to state that while he objects to the extraordinary charge demanded for the safe carriage of Coal from Dublin to Dromod by the Midland Great Western Railway Company, he considers that it is better to subject to the extortion than to lose a large quantity of Coal in transit as happened last year".

The letter has all the hallmarks of Lord Leitrim's style: pragmatic, curmudgeonly, and insisting on having the last word.

Neither did his family escape his directives. On the baptism of a grand-niece in 1875, he wrote sarcastically to Robert and Winifred with a suggestion that invited immediate obeisance: "in addition to your poetical Hilda may I suggest that you introduce the word Mary after Robert's grandmother". His irritation with his nephew is barely veiled in his letters to

Robert and his wife. In early 1878, Robert was foolish enough to tell his uncle about a current dilemma: the response is cutting: "if your mind is so mixed up between taking a farm of 80 acres and going abroad to amuse yourself . . . it must be in a rather chotic [sic] condition."

Whatever one's opinion of the man, it is difficult not to accept his deep sense of duty and ownership of his lands and tenants. Letters by Lord Leitrim's clerk and agent, William Rose, record a huge amount of building and maintenance work throughout the estate and ongoing purchase, movement and sale of livestock between Rynn, Killadoon and Donegal. Cattle were driven as far as Strabane for sale (one "Fat Heifer" sold for £14.10.0 at one fair there) though most went only as far as Mohill fair. In 1855, Lord Leitrim was apparently satisfied with getting £3.2.6 each for three "very nice" yearling heifers and a total of £60 for seven cows. And he insisted on the best treatment for his cattle. Once, when he noticed that some of his 'Devon Calves' were "unwell", he wrote identical letters to Francis Noble and George Latimer directing them both to come to Lough Rynn the following afternoon to inspect the cattle.

When Lord Leitrim was away from Lough Rynn—mostly visiting his other estates in Killadoon and Donegal—his agent wrote weekly letters keeping His Lordship informed of the estate. Each letter contained an estimate of the wage bill and general expenditure for the current week and usually an acknowledgement of payment received for the previous week's estimate, which averaged at £40-£60.

A letter from his agent, William Rose, in June 1855, is not unusual in the detail, range and industry it describes.

> Lough Rynn
> June 28th 1855
>
> I beg to enclose to your Lordship the Estimate for the present week.
>
> I have received your Lordship's Letter of the 23rd Inst and in reply beg to acquaint you that we have arranged with Connor Heslin to drive the cows to Killadoon and to bring back the Swans, he is to take his Jennet and Cart with him as far as Mullingar and leave it there until he returns from Maynooth, he is to leave Lough Rynn on Monday next the 2nd July. I have written to the Station Master at Mullingar for a Time and Fare Table, when I receive I shall write to Mr Dow to ask him to send a man with the Swans to meet Heslin at Maynooth and to drive the Cattle to Killadoon so that Heslin will have to go no farther than Maynooth.
>
> We have rec'd the Furniture from Messrs Kerrs, Dublin.
>
> The Eaves Gutters have not yet arrived. I have Roarke the Mason employed to make the stone at the Church by day's wages. I have made an agreement with him to Rough cast the Walls of the Church, to mix the mortar and find his own attendance for £1.18.0 subject to your Lordship's approval.
>
> The Cottages in Cashill and Derraun are now all finished, and Masterson and the Thatcher are now repairing the Cottage at Clooncarne, formerly held by Hopkins.

> The Horse "Peter" (Mulvey) appears to be much better, his eyes are much clearer but they are running a little yet. Dr Dobson has given Mathew some medicine for him and a wash for his eyes.
>
> Leyt Rogers has joined the reg't at Longford and his Wife is living at the Gate House until your Lordship will give some direction about another family being placed there. Sergt Major Costelloes family are to leave Rynn this week. His son Charles says he will go and enlist in the Reg't but McManus says he will not permit him to go away without first paying all that is due to him as his Master, or if he will not Pay he must stay during the Term of his Apprenticeship.
>
> The Stock are all doing well and Mr Leckies has commenced mowing in Clooncoo, as the weather is now very favourable.
>
> I am My Lord
> Your Lordship's Most Obedient Servant
> William Rose Jr.
>
> The Right Hon'ble The Earl of Leitrim

Evictions

Evictions, or ejectments, are recorded on the Lough Rynn Estate from the 1840s on. Some are recorded during the Famine but not huge numbers. However, by the late 1840s, many evictions were carried out for non-payment of rent during those famine years.

In June 1849, a Bailiff for Lough Rynn, Richard Mayne of Monaghan issued a Warrant to evict twenty-nine tenants for rents owed "up to and for" the 29th September 1847. Mayne appointed James Maguinis of Rouskeynamona and his assistants to "take, lead, drive, carry away, and dispose of" the tenants' homes and their contents to satisfy "rent due and payable to the Right Honorable the Earl of Leitrim".

The affected tenants were all from the townlands of Errew, Farnaught, Gortletteragh, Gortnalamph and Rouskeynamona and included:

Hugh Reynolds
James Bohan
Thomas Cannon
Peter Mulligan
Pat Bohan
Widow Reynolds
James Fanning
Owen Reynolds
Bryan Reynolds
Widow of Anthony Beirne
Alick Balain
Peter Reynolds
James Beirne
Thomas Lion
Peter Diffley
Thomas Lion
Pat Mulligan
Bryan McDermott
James Mulloy
Pat Hanford
Widow Bridget McDermott 1st
Widow Bridget McDermott 2nd
Laughlin McGarry
Pat Reynolds
Daniel Reynolds
Michael Conboy
Dennis Beirne
Hugh Reynolds
James Lowry

The Warrant was followed up with a Notice of Distress for Rent, issued to each individual which stated the consequences of non-payment in unequivocal terms: ". . . and unless said Rent and the Charges of such Distress be paid within Fourteen Days from the date hereof, the Goods and Chattels so Distrained will be disposed of according to Law for the satisfaction of such Rent and charges." While these Warrants and Notices were issued in the name of the Earl of Leitrim, Clement's father, we can assume they were issued on the orders of Lord Clements who was very much in charge of things at Lough Rynn. The evictions started mostly as Lord Leitrim's way of imposing his own rights and privileges on his estates: the idea that tenants might have the right to improve their holdings at their own will was anathema to him. By the late 1850s, his evictions had won notoriety for their indiscriminate nature and were in most cases ordered to accomplish land improvements such as creating new plantations of trees or "for the purpose of revising the townland". He is said to have issued "lavish and pitiless notices to quit", going so far as to print them on the backs of rent receipts. Unlike some of his peers, Lord Leitrim showed no nepotism to Protestant farmers, and was as likely to order their eviction as he was their Catholic neighbours.

In November 1850, twelve houses were demolished on one day by the sub-sheriff and a posse. The tenants had held the land for only two years and had inherited arrears of cess and poor rates. They offered to pay a year's rent there and then, but the bailiff refused it and called for the evictions to go ahead. Nine families were made homeless at one of the worst times of the year. It was alleged that the bailiff acted without the sanction of Clements or the 2nd Earl, to whom the land belonged. Even if true, Clements' reputation and record would indicate support for the act.

The evictions after the Famine were driven from a different compulsion. The economic benefits of a land cleared of small-holders and conacre tenants were obvious, and there was no reason not to take full advantage of his power to accelerate the change.

I, RICHARD MAYNE, of *Newbliss*, in the County of *Monaghan*, Agent of the Right Honorable the EARL of LEITRIM, do hereby Nominate, Constitute, and Appoint ~~of~~ and JAMES MAGUINIS, of *Rouskeyamona*, in the County of *Leitrim*, and their Assistants, for me, and in my name, within Twenty Days from the Date hereof, to Enter and Distrain, ALL THAT AND THOSE, that part of the lands of Eneor Tamnaght, Gortleteragh, Gortnelamph and Rouskeyamona in the occupation of Hugh Reynolds, James Bohan, Thomas Cannon, Peter Mulligan, Pat Bohan, Reps. Widow Reynolds, James Fanning, Owen Reynolds, Bryan Reynolds, Widow of Anthony Beirne, Hugh Balam, Peter Reynolds, James Beirne, Thomas Iron, Peter Diffley, Thos. Iron, Pat Mulligan, Bryan McDermott, James Mulloy, Widow Bruagel McDermott 1st and Widow Bruagel McDermot 2nd, Laughlin McGarry and Tim McDermott, Pat Hanley and [illegible], Pat Reynolds [illegible] Reynolds, Michl. Comboy, Dennis [illegible] and the Distress and Distresses there found, to take, lead, drive, carry away, and the same to Dispose of according to Law, to satisfy the ~~Sum of~~ ~~Pounds,~~ ~~Shillings, and~~ ~~Pence,~~ Rent due and payable to the Right Honorable the EARL of LEITRIM, out of said Premises, by the said several parties, before named

up to and for the 29th day of Sept. One Thousand, Eight Hundred, and Forty-~~Eight~~ Seven together with the Costs and Charges of such Distress, for which this shall be their sufficient Warrant and Authority.

In Witness whereof, I have hereunto Signed my Name, this 20th day of ~~May~~ June One Thousand, Eight Hundred, and Forty-Nine

At *Mohill*, in the County of *Leitrim*.

Richd. Mayne SEAL

Fig. 36: Notice of Distress for Rent in 1849, evicting 29 tenants

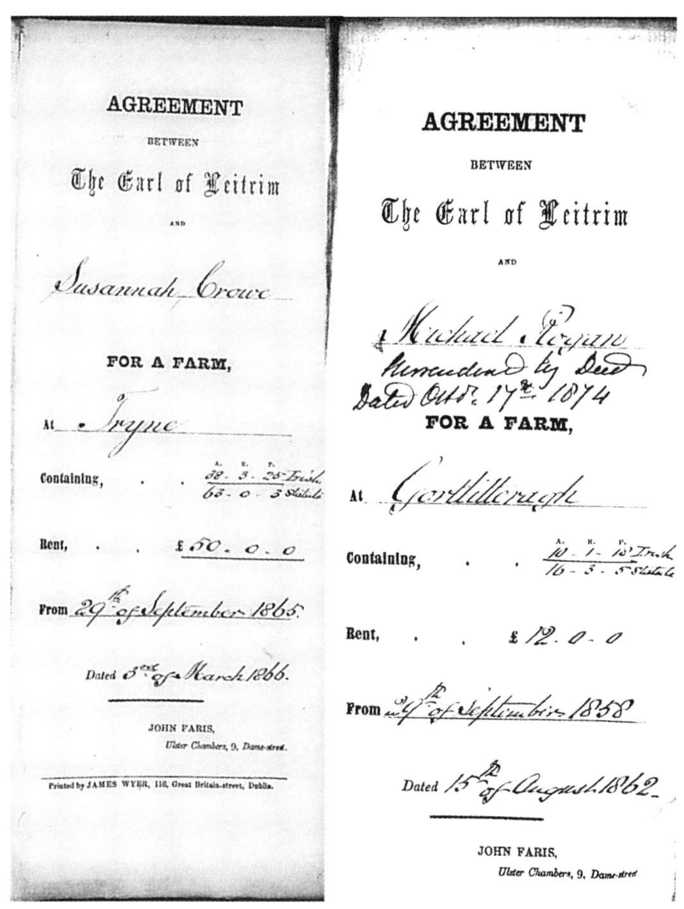

AGREEMENT

BETWEEN

The Earl of Leitrim

AND

Susannah Crowe

FOR A FARM,

At Tryne

Containing, A. R. P. 38 - 3 - 25 Irish / 63 - 0 - 3 Statute

Rent, £50 . 0 . 0

From 29th of September 1865.

Dated 3rd of March 1866.

JOHN FARIS,
Ulster Chambers, 9, Dame-street.

Printed by JAMES WYER, 116, Great Britain-street, Dublin.

AGREEMENT

BETWEEN

The Earl of Leitrim

AND

Michael Rogan
Surrendered by Deed
Dated Octr. 17th 1874

FOR A FARM,

At Gortletteragh

Containing, A. R. P. 10 - 1 - 10 Irish / 16 - 3 - 5 Statute

Rent, £12 . 0 . 0

From 29th of September 1858

Dated 15th of August 1862.

JOHN FARIS,
Ulster Chambers, 9, Dame-street.

Fig. 37: Rental Agreements

Covers of two rental agreements with Lord Leitrim, one with Susannah Crowe for a farm at Tryne in 1865; the other with Michael Rogan for a farm at Gortletteragh dated 1858. © National Library of Ireland. Reprinted with permission.

Notice of Distress for Rent.

To be delivered or posted where Distress is made by Agent or Bailiff.—9 and 10 Victoria, c. 111, s. 10.

TAKE NOTICE, that I have this day entered and made a Distress for Rent on ALL THAT AND THOSE,

for the Sum of £ 6 : 15 : 0 , being the amount of the Rent demanded, and the time and times when the same accrued due, are as follow, viz. :—

£	s.	d.			
6	15	0	due and ending the 25th	day of March	1847
:	:		due and ending the	day of	18
:	:		due and ending the	day of	18
:	:		due and ending the	day of	18

And I have made such Distress by the Authority of

the Landlord of said Premises, and party entitled to the said Rent; and unless said Rent, and the Charges of such Distress be paid within Fourteen Days from the date hereof, the Goods and Chattels so Distrained, will be disposed of according to Law, for satisfaction of such Rent and charges.

Dated this 7th day of Sept 1849

of

in the County of Leitrim

To Wid Ellen Reynolds.
the person, or persons, in possession of the said premises.

TURNER, PRINTER, MOHILL.

Fig. 38: Notice of Distress for Rent

The Notice, dated 7th September 1849, gives notice to Widow Ellen Reynolds that unless she pays the £6/15/0 owed in rent within fourteen days the land, "goods and chattels" will be re-possessed. © National Library of Ireland. Reprinted with permission.

The Earl had long thought the land over-populated and the small farms unsustainable: now he had validation of his hypothesis. The new spate of evictions were less about non-payment during the Famine, but about increased productivity and agricultural progress. In ways it harked back to the 1830s when the Clements' despaired of the ability of the tenants to make good the land (not acknowledging that penalties for improvement and high rents for land they considered theirs were hardly inducements to improvement). Forty years later, the reformist zeal remained, but despair had turned to contempt.

By 1861, he may have even begun to refuse new tenants. In a letter dated January 1861, he wrote that he was not looking to let land, preferring to turn existing lessees into "good working farms".

> Lough Rynn, Mohill
> 21 January 1861
>
> Dear Sir,
>
> I am unable to read your writing but believe the subject of your letter is something reflecting the Letting of Land. I am not prepared to Let any at present – and until I have found that which is in my own -- into good working farms, it is not my instruction to look for a Tenant.
>
> Faithfully yours, L.

He did, however, around this time formalise and renew a number of tenancies. Tenant agreements were printed to reflect the new arrangements. (Interestingly, while Lord Leitrim had a reputation as a misogynist, quite a few of his lessees were women: in 1866, Susannah Crowe signed a lease for sixty-three statute acres at Treanmore.)

After 1855, evictions affected less that one-quarter per cent of all agricultural tenants in Ireland. Lord Leitrim stands out, as Hoppen puts it, precisely because of their rarity. However, Hoppen also discriminates between the number of eviction notices issued that were "scattered like confetti" as against the number that were actually implemented. Also, there is evidence that not all those evicted were rendered homeless: at least some were placed in new smallholdings with lower rent and in some cases a better quality house. In 1866, a Nicholas Doyle was evicted from his home at Laheen South for non-payment of rent. He was moved to one of the earl's farms in Clooncarne that carried a lower rent while his original farm was handed over to a man named French from County Cavan. Similarly, in 1874, the Earl's bailiff, Arthur Scott, evicted Michael Rogan of Gortletteragh for non-payment of rent and installed him in a cottage "lately occupied by John Glancy a servant and caretaker to the Earl". Scott notes that Rogan's original house was "in a very bad state and likely to fall". Essentially, tenants who were not up to standard (for whatever reason) were arbitrarily replaced by hand-picked tenants who, in Lord Leitrim's view, were more likely to turn the land into "a good working farm". Most of the Earl's land was held on an 'At Will' or 'year-to-year' basis, rather than the 21-year leases that had been common earlier. This was the case in Rogan's displacement and clearly made the eviction process easier for the Earl while causing great uncertainty for the tenants. (In Doyle's case, there was an alleged prurient interest by the Earl in Mr French's daughter.) In addition to the new lease terms, the rents also rose substantially. As if the mutability of the lease was not enough, the rent increases proved impossible for many tenants: an increase from £12 to £18 for a ten-acre farm required an unusual level of husbandry to turn a profit, even with a good market for produce, and for many tenants was quite beyond their means.

1824	9 acres; annual rent £11/3/8; lease for life of queen or 21 years
1855	9 acres; 'at will'
1856	Rent raised from £12/12 to £18
1877	Holding surrendered for the purpose of revising the townland

In 1858, Lord Leitrim ordered an eviction which The Nation, the widely read newspaper of the nationalist Young Irelanders, believed could have had dire consequences. Lord Leitrim ordered that the Church at Gortletteragh be repossessed for non-payment of rent. In doing so, he overturned his father's decision not to take rent for the site.

When the parish priest refused to vacate the church, he was served with a notice to quit. On the appointed day, the church was repossessed with a force of a thousand men, comprising police and military with fixed bayonets and crowbars. Six thousand men turned out to resist the possession, coming from Longford, Roscommon and Westmeath as well as from all over Leitrim. The event, however, passed peacefully, due apparently to the diplomacy and negotiation skills of the parish priest. In the end, Lord Leitrim capitulated somewhat, ordering rent to be paid for the land around the church, but not for the church itself. Apparently this story caused little surprise in the country. The tone of The Nation's report on the story reflected a resigned acceptance of the events. It reported that Lord Leitrim was "already famous for such proceedings towards his tenantry as not many even of his own order dare imitate".

Resentment continued to grow. In the 1860s Lord Leitrim was the target of several assassination attempts. In September 1860, the Earl was fired at in Mohill, though this incident had little to do with land and evictions. The Earl had just finished attending a meeting in the workhouse and was turning into Main Street. As he turned the corner, a loud explosion was heard and witnesses could see dense smoke coming from James Murphy's shop some forty yards away on the other side of the street. The Leitrim Gazette reported that Lord Leitrim continued walking down the street "unawed", as if nothing untoward had happened. Two policemen ran immediately into the shop and found James Murphy with a blunderbuss, a loaded pistol, two daggers and an amount of ammunition. Two days earlier, Murphy had sent a note to Lord Leitrim challenging him to a duel at Cullinan's crossroads to "take satisfaction for your ruffianly conduct towards my wife". Lord Leitrim evidently ignored the note and experienced the consequences. Murphy was arrested and sentenced to transportation. He was later reprieved by the Lord Lieutenant, Carlisle, on grounds of insanity and ordered to be detained in an asylum. It transpired that the man had a habit of challenging anybody who spoke with his wife, believing them to have some nefarious interest.

Lord Leitrim was disgusted with the reduced sentence and became even more disenchanted with the government. He was particularly infuriated with Carlisle and had one of his most spectacular and public rows with him. As well as holding Carlisle responsible for much of the Liberals' incompetence during the Famine; Lord Leitrim also disliked him personally, though the two had been friends at one time.

It says something about Lord Leitrim's character that three years later, he sought an opportunity to extract revenge. When he heard that Carlisle was travelling to Galway and intended staying at the Maam Hotel, he directed the inn-keeper (a tenant) to fill the hotel with tenants and workmen so that not a room would be free for Carlisle. Instead of scoring a petty victory, Lord Leitrim was assailed on all sides as a spiteful, crusty, eccentric old man. Carlisle retaliated by stripping Lord Leitrim of his posts as Justice of the Peace for Leitrim, Donegal and Galway—an action that was applauded in most quarters. In London, the satirical magazine Punch reported the story, treating it as the farce it was:

The Noble Earl of Leitrim, being an Irish Landlord, has of course been shot at: but although a man of some mark he had the fortune to be missed. It is the opinion of his Lordship that the Irish Government omitted duly to punish the author of the outrage which he experienced.

To this impression on the mind of Lord Leitrim is ascribed the subjoined letter, which that nobleman wrote to one of his vassals, keeper of the Maam Hotel, in the Western Highlands of Ireland, through which Her Majesty's Lord Lieutenant, the Earl of Carlisle happened to be journeying at the time on a tour of inspection: –

> *King. I will be obliged to you to fill the hotel with my tenants forthwith. Let every room be occupied immediately, and continue to be occupied; and when so occupied, you will refuse admittance to Lord Carlisle and his party. If there should be the slightest difficulty as to filling the hotel, or the occupation of the rooms, my desire is that you will fill each room with the workmen; but you must not admit Lord Carlisle, and consequently the rooms should be occupied previous to his coming there, any orders you may have received notwithstanding. I rely on your observing my wishes to the letter. Yours faithfully, Leitrim*
>
> *P.S. I will pay for the tenants using the rooms.*

Fig. 39: Punch, 24th October 1863 "The Earl of Leitrim's Revenge"

Back at home, Lord Leitrim's distrust of the administration and the courts increased. In a response to a letter from his agent, George West, he writes:

> "I thank you for your kind congratulations at my recent escape from assassination and being made the victim of Political Conspiracy, but at the same time I must observe that the best way to prevent crime is to carry the Law into effect.
>
> And I was very sorry to learn that recently when two men were brought before the Bench in Mohill for being in arms in a Proclaimed district, the Bench [ ] dismissed the case and ordered the arms to be returned which was clearly contrary to law. I would recommend you when any such matter should occur and where you are in doubt as to the law to postpone the Court until you are better informed, and not to trust what may be stated by the defendants."

In early 1861, The Irishman journal called him "an incarnate terror to the Irish tenant". By the 1870s, Lord Leitrim was said to symbolise "evil at its worst". In parliament, from the 1860s, he had ceased to support the Liberals and voted with the Conservatives. In 1870, he spoke vociferously against

Gladstone's Land Act[30] in the House of Lords, believing it to be a gross encroachment on his rights as a landlord; he was one of only eight peers who voted against it. The Act went against everything that the Earl now stood for. (However, it did contain one important loophole: tenants who had to vacate their land because their leases had expired were not covered by the Act: Lord Leitrim and others exploited this by forcing tenants to accept restrictive leases.)

The Earl became increasingly isolated. In the House of Lords, his few friends finally deserted him after he presented false statistics relating to crime in Leitrim in a petition against agrarian outrage. The figures were proven untrue by the local magistrates. In a rare note of despondency, in July 1873, the Earl wrote to his nephew Robert (before said nephew was disinherited) that "I regard my estates as a burden too heavy to bear and I wish to dispose of them . . . Ireland is no long a country that it is desirable to live in or to have any property in." This particular instance had been sparked by his reported theft of £1,588—"with the prospect of other serious losses".

---

30 The 1870 Land Act introduced some protection for tenants: if they were evicted, tenants would receive limited compensation if they had made improvements or if they were evicted for reasons other than non-payment of rent. The Act also made limited provision for occupying tenants to purchase land.

Lord Leitrim assassinated

Over the decades, Lord Leitrim showed no signs of slowing down or tempering his hands-on style. He travelled to fairs as far away as Ballinasloe or Strabane to buy his own cattle and livestock. He collected rents in person and personally discharged or engaged workmen. His hand-written notes on 'Proposals for Land' or on tenders for building work all demonstrate his eye for detail and need to be at the centre of his affairs. The week before his assassination, Lord Leitrim was in Dublin ordering seeds for the estate. On being told it would take a week for the order to be completed, he replied, somewhat prophetically, "A week! Where may I be within a week?"

Although he made Lough Rynn his principal seat, Lord Leitrim frequently travelled to his estates in Kildare, Donegal and Galway, and paid occasional visits to Dublin. In 1878, at 72 years of age, he was still physically strong, though increasingly irascible. In Donegal especially, his eviction policy and general treatment of tenants had gained him serious enemies, and he was forced to travel heavily armed and with a strong escort. Wholesale evictions ordered in 1878, were said to be the final straw.

In Milford, Donegal, three men decided to take matters into their own hands. On the morning of 2nd April 1878, Michael Heraghty, Michael McElwee and Neil Sheils ambushed and killed Lord Leitrim at Cratlagh Wood, near Milford. It was a well-planned attack: the assassins were aware of Lord Leitrim's movements and knew exactly when and how he would be travelling from his home. The three men arrived at Cratlagh Wood at 7 o'clock and waited patiently for their target.

The Earl was nothing if not predictable. He rose early, so that he could be in Milford by nine o'clock and he had given his usual orders for his servant and luggage to be taken from his house at Manorvaughan to Milford. By this time, it was known that the Earl was a marked man and the local constabulary had made it a habit to accompany him to Milford. His friends had warned him not to be so venturesome and never to go unarmed.

> It was well known that the deceased nobleman was for a long time past a marked man and in consequence of this it was customary for the Milford police to go out to Manorvaughan when it was known that his Lordship was coming. On the morning of the outrage, the constabulary would have been at the scene of the murder in time had not his Lordship left an hour earlier than he had intended previously. *Londonderry Journal, 5 April 1878*

Lord Leitrim set out an hour earlier than scheduled—without his police escort. It was said afterwards that the clocks in Manorvaughan had been deliberately set back. There may be some truth in this: Lord Leitrim was a stickler for punctuality and it would be unusual for his to vary so much from a plan. He was also courageous—or careless—and would not have felt obliged to wait for the constables. As John Madden said afterwards of one of his last conversations with the Earl, "he was a man who did not know what fear was and never took the slightest precaution". As it happens, the Earl did take the precaution of carrying two guns on this journey. He had a loaded, double-chambered pocket pistol under his overcoat and another heavy revolver in a black bag tied to the driver's seat.

Fig. 40: Punch cartoon July 1878, depicting the assassination of Lord Leitrim

The caption on the original read: "'Waiting for the landlord!', by Charles Keene, 1878: 'Sure, Tirince, I hope the ould gintleman hasn't mit wid an accidint!!!'"

It couldn't have been a pleasant journey. It was bitterly cold with strong icy winds and driving sleet showers. Lord Leitrim and the others were well wrapped up in heavy coats and horse blankets. The road from Manorvaughan to Milford has a dip at Cratlagh Wood that rises to a steep hill: the horses had to slow to a trudging walk, and were slowed further by the biting wind and sleet. There were two cars in the party: the first was the Milford Hotel coach carrying Lord Leitrim, the Court Clerk John Makim, and a young coachman Charles Buchanan; the second car held Lord Leitrim's coachman and valet, William Kincaid, and Michael Logue, the owner and driver of the car. Whether by accident or design, this car was slowed down with a heavy load of the Earl's luggage and by having a lame horse. Coming some 200 meters behind the first car, Kincaid had a full view of the ambush which he later described to the courts.

The first Kincaid knew of the incident was a report from a volley of several shots below him on the road. Looking towards the sound, he saw jets of smoke from the guns. Charles Buchanan had been shot in the head and died immediately. He fell to the road, his rug still around his knees. John Makim, the clerk, was also shot in the head but managed to stumble back towards the second car: he died later.

Lord Leitrim never got a chance to get to either of his weapons. One of the first shots hit him in the right arm, fracturing his elbow joint and he took nine or ten bullets in the back of his left shoulder. The frightened horses panicked and Lord Leitrim fell to the ground. McElwee and Shiels approached, no doubt to check that he was dead. But the Earl managed to get to his feet and wrestle with the two: when he was found later, he was still clutching a portion of a red beard belonging to McElwee. The struggle was short, and ended when Shiels struck Lord Leitrim with the butt of a gun in a blow that was violent enough to split the gunstock. After dumping the body face down in a pool of water close-by, the two assassins fled. We can only assume that the combination of heavy overcoat and fractured elbow prevented the Earl from getting to either of his weapons. His new hat was found on the road, unsoiled and unbattered. The black bag full of money and containing the fine revolver was left intact.

Shiels and McElwee ran to the shores of Mulroy Bay to a waiting boat: Kincaid watched them row hurriedly from the shore and disappear across the bay.

The broken gunstock was the only evidence left behind and provided proof against only one of the conspirators, Michael Heraghty. As it happened, Heraghty had left the scene earlier to follow a pedestrian who had passed the three as they took up their positions on the road. Suspecting that the passer-by might have noticed something amiss and afraid that he might warn the authorities in Milford, Heraghty was chosen to shadow the man and ensure he proved no threat. He left his gun behind and it was this that was used to inflict the fatal blow. Why Heraghty was chosen to leave is a mystery. Of the three, he was reputed to be the best shot, a skill he had refined through his main occupation, poaching.

There was little doubt among the tenantry about who the actual assassins were, but no one informed the police.

Immediately after the murder, each of the conspirators went back about their daily business. McElwee was to be seen soon afterwards constructing lobster pots and Shiels went back to his tailor shop. Heraghty went to the house of some friends where he had a meal of tea and eggs.

In the end, Heraghty was the only one to be arrested. He appeared at Lifford Assizes on 19th July, 1878. He was described as being about twenty years of age, small and wiry with black hair, light grey eyes and a low forehead. On the day of his trial, he was "sallow and ill-looking". He died in gaol three months later from typhus and without being convicted for the crime. Aside from Heraghty, the local constabulary arrested four other tenants, Bernard, Pat and Anthony McGrenahan, and Charles McEntaggart. They also arrested one Manus Trainor, whose only incriminating action had been to book a passage on an emigrant ship some time before the assassination. Large sums were collected locally for the defence, but the five were soon discharged for lack of evidence.

Of the three men ultimately attributed with Lord Leitrim's murder, two died before they could come to trial; the third, McElwee, was never apprehended and continued his career as a travelling tailor until his death in 1921.

Robert Clements, the Earl's nephew and prospective heir, was in Paris when he got word of the assassination: he and his wife abandoned their planned journey to Italy and set off immediately for Dublin to attend the funeral in St. Michan's Church.

Lord Leitrim's body had been taken to Killadoon in Kildare, and from there made its way in a regal procession towards Dublin. By the time the funeral cortège reached Dublin, word had spread of the Earl's death. The procession along the Liffey was marked by unruly scenes with locals hurling abuse as the coffin passed. John Burges, Lord Leitrim's brother-in-law, and Robert Clements were astounded at the size and anger of the mob that heckled the cortège and threatened to seize the coffin. In the end, Robert Clements feared the crowd so much that he insisted on being the only person to accompany the coffin as it was interred in the family vault inside the church. During the funeral service, there was yet another contrasting view of the Earl's character: the Dean noted, that for St. Michan's at least, Lord Leitrim's "purse was ever open" and the Earl had recently given a large donation towards the renovation of Handel's organ and £100 to the curate endowment fund.

In seeking a rationale for the assassination, it was reported that, in addition to the evictions, the final straw was an accusation that Lord Leitrim had debauched a young servant girl, a daughter of one of the assassins. There are conflicting stories of Lord Leitrim's treatment of women on his estates: some say that he repeatedly violated young girls and claimed 'droit de seigneur'; others refute this, saying that he treated women with respect, but mostly ignored them.

Even some of his peers repeated accusations of his immorality towards daughters of tenants in the House of Commons and named him "the bad earl".

Fig. 41: Cover from 'The Third Earl'

Pictured are 1) Lord Leitrim; 2) William Kincaid, Lord Leitrim's coachman and valet; 3) John Makim, a Court Clerk; 4) Michael Logue, the owner and driver of the car; 5) Charles Buchanan, a young coachman. Makim and Buchanan also died in the ambush.

Ten days after his death, Frank Hugh O'Donnell, MP, a colleague of Parnell's alleged in the House of Commons that the cause of the murder was Leitrim's "acts of sexual immorality" on his Donegal property. He declared that "if it could be proved that this man was the terror of the countryside, a notorious evictor and a notorious lecher, then that man deserved to die". At that point King-Harman rose and declared "I see strangers". The House was cleared of the 'Strangers', including journalists and members of the public and the debate continued in camera. The Hansard report for that day merely records "The debate then continued for some hours". We will never know if O'Donnell produced evidence to substantiate his allegations.

But an authoritative journalist investigating his assassination wrote "even among those who hold the strongest views upon Lord Leitrim's conduct as a landlord, the charge (of debauchery) is discredited and I did not meet a single person who regarded it as tenable". Others also refuted the charge, saying that he treated women with respect, but mostly ignored them. A stable boy employed by the Earl remembered him as a "woman hater" and that he, Kane, "never knew him to have anything to do with any of them".

Later, a local observer described Lord Leitrim as having alienated the local Donegal population "not so much by certain immoralities", as by his heavy-handed disregard for his tenants: "he used to go into the houses and pull down cartoons and placards, if he saw them put up on the walls", and as ever showed no favour to any religious party: he would pull down King William and the Pope with "an equal hand".

Rewards offered

Various rewards were offered for the identification of Lord Leitrim's killers. The heir to the earldom, Robert Clements, offered £10,000. A group of thirty magistrates meeting a week after the killing passed a resolution to raise a subscription as a reward for the arrest of the assassins. A few allies contributed £6,000 to the fund, led by a single contribution of £1,000 by the Duke of Abercorn. A £500 reward was offered by the government: this carried the condition that information had to be submitted within six months—not a great indication of any enthusiasm to apprehend the assassins. Officially, no information was forthcoming and the rewards went unclaimed. However, in the 1960s, it emerged that information had, in fact, been gained by the Lord Lieutenant's agent (for seventeen shillings), but it had been filed away in Dublin Castle and was never referred to. The truth was, Lord Leitrim was mourned by neither tenants nor peers. Only Mr. King-Harman (of nearby Roscommon and MP for Sligo) spoke in the House of Commons in Lord Leitrim's defence, and this was to jeers and heckling from the other members. The Earl's killers were lauded locally as heroes who ended the tyranny of landlordism in Ireland. The assassination was seen as a landmark in the fight for tenants' rights and is widely believed to have given impetus to the Land League which was founded by Michael Davitt the following year.

Back at Lough Rynn, the Castle received a number of letters from some of the Earl's larger lease-holders noting their regret at his death. A large meeting was held in Mohill, led by two of the Earl's principal tenants, his doctor and solicitor. Seventy farmers attended and signed a letter of condolence that included a denial of all scandalous stories about the Earl. Instead, the letter noted that "No man did more for his tenantry than Lord Leitrim did. His chief aim was for their welfare." Few, if any, expressions of regret were received from tenants on smallholdings. Only the Orange Lodge in Mohill seemed to regret sincerely Lord Leitrim's passing. After a meeting in Mohill Courthouse, they issued a statement declaring that the Lodge's members "sing the praises of Lord Leitrim, and proclaim to the world that he was a chaste God-fearing man and a kind indulgent landlord and that anyone who would say otherwise are traitors". Most of the people of Lough Rynn at least seemed to be at one in mourning the twenty-three-year-old John Makim who was shot with the Earl. The young clerk had only recently moved to Milford from Rynn. His funeral cortège was met outside Mohill by a "vast number" of tenantry and estate employees, and shops closed until the "beautiful, solemn burial service" was concluded.

After his death, the legacy and memory of Lord Leitrim focused squarely on his darker side and on the real and perceived hardships endured by his tenants. The songs, ballads and stories that prevailed into the twentieth century, told only of a tyrannical landlord and notorious despot. 'The Banks of Mulroy Bay' concludes its six verses with:

> The great exterminator; the Lord of this estate,
> For him there was an inch of lead—too hard to masticate.
> His body it lay lifeless on the road, I heard them say,
> To feed the dogs and hungry crows on the banks of Mulroy Bay.

In a similar vein, 'The Shooting of Lord Leitrim' calls on the "men of Leitrim" to rejoice in the death of the "hoary sinner" who held them in serfdom and slavery:

> The widow's prayers he laughed at;
> The orphans' tears despised.
> He rooted up their homesteads
> And in poverty they died.
> He trampled on their sacred rights
> That earned their sweated toil,
> And he banished them in hundreds
> From Tirconaill's holy soil.

After Lord Leitrim

The most likely heir to Lord Leitrim's lands and title was his nephew, Robert Bermingham Clements. Robert had maintained a relatively good relationship with his uncle, but (apart from naming his children incorrectly) had caused concern with his choice of wife and perceived lack of interest in the management of his estates. The Earl had urged Robert to marry an Irish woman, like Lady Rossmore's daughter, apparently fearing that an English wife would want to live in England, thus rendering Robert an absentee landlord. Not a desirable state of affairs. Heedless of his uncle's admonishments, Robert did marry an English Lady, Winifred Coke, fifth daughter of Thomas Coke, 2nd Earl of Leicester.

Having rushed to attend the funeral of his uncle, and having offered a substantial reward for the capture of the assassins, the heir apparent was shocked to hear that he had been disinherited in 1876: all the lands were to go to a second cousin of Lord Leitrim; Robert would inherit only the title.

The new Earl was not the only person to be surprised by the Will. When he learned of the revised terms, one of the trustees of the Will, George A. Hill of Ramelton remarked, "I am so astonished at what you have told me that I can hardly believe that my poor friend was in his right senses".

Indeed it seems that Lord Leitrim had fallen out with most of his relatives, and although he could do nothing about the hereditary title, he left all his property in Leitrim, Donegal, Galway and Kildare, to a second cousin, Colonel Henry Theophilus Clements of Ashfield Lodge, Co. Cavan.

Commenting on the whole scenario in a letter dated 23 April 1878, the Countess of Dartrey wrote:

> "In this country we have yet hardly recovered the horror of poor Lord Leitrim's murder, which in savagery exceeds any crime committed since I have known Ireland. So much for the message of peace! His will is a most cruel one by his nephew and successor in the title, as he only gets a small entailed property of £1,400 or £1,500 a year. Everything else (I should think at least £18,000 a year in property and £90,000 of money) is left to trustees for the benefit of the late Lord's third cousin, Colonel H. Clements, and his heirs male, failing these to a son of the present Lord's second sister, a Mrs Madden of this county. Her husband is a semi-madman, who stood as a Tory Home Ruler for Monaghan in 1868, and wrote such outrageous letters that he was struck off the list of J.Ps. Colonel Clements is a near neighbour of ours and intimate friend, nearly sixty; a most excellent man, although a dull one. He has only one delicate

> boy, and was utterly taken by surprise and much vexed by the will, and would fain resign part at least of the property, but the remainders will, it is feared, make it impossible. Lord Leitrim's first will left all to his nephew. A later one superseded this and left it as above, and a later one still is in existence, but alas not signed, again leaving all to his nephew. I hear the present Lord and his wife are bearing the disappointment most admirably."

Displaying a degree of amiability and compromise that had not been evident in their relative, the two heirs reached agreement within a year of the murder: the Colonel, clearly seeing the unfairness of the Will, agreed that Robert, the 4th Earl, should take the Donegal estates. Two Acts of Parliament, the Leitrim Estate Acts of 1879 and 1880, were needed to legalise the arrangement.

The 3rd Earl had also disinherited his brother Charles and sisters Maria and Elizabeth. Only with his sister Caroline's family did he act in any way graciously, if one can believe his brother-in-law's defence of him. The sons of the Earl's niece, Lady Caroline Madden also had a claim on the estates: all would revert to them should Colonel Clements die without issue. Their father, John Madden felt obliged to protect his children's interest and commenced litigation. Under the 1880 Act, Robert Clements agreed to compensate the Maddens with £5,000. The disputes over the estate continued, and there was a further settlement in 1893 when £5,000 was distributed to the Maddens and £30,000 divided in four portions between the 3rd Earl's siblings or their issue: Lady

Marie Keppel, Lady Elizabeth V. Clements, the seven children of Rev. F N Clements, and the three children of Lady Caroline Burges. The only other people for whom the Earl retained some regard were, it seems, his loyal servants: in his will, he left £1,000 to his housekeeper May Heneghan and £20 to each of his female servants. He bequeathed £200 to William Kincaid, the coachman who had been in the Earl's service for 22 years and who had witnessed the assassination.[31]

As it happens, Lord Leitrim did Robert an injustice. Winifred, as predicted, did not like Ireland and spent most of her time in London (coming to live in Mulroy only a few years before her death). The 4th Earl, however, went on to improve greatly the position of the tenants on the Donegal estates. Immediately after the killing, the Earl was seen riding alone between Milford and Manorvaughan in an attempt to demonstrate his confidence in the tenantry. In a more salient gesture, he indicated his intention to undertake improvements around the estate and issued a declaration that arbitrary evictions would stop and that tenants would be supplied with seed to crop their land. He noted pragmatically, "without crops you cannot expect rents". By August, he had offered to review rents and consider the question of 'free sale'. Each tenant was allocated a portion of bog and guaranteed it would be his until it lasted. In a complete

---

31 In 'Portrait of the Artist as a Young Man', James Joyce uses the term "Lord Leitrim's coachman" to refer to a person who was more subservient and loyal to England than to Ireland.

reversal of the 3rd Earl's approach, the new landlord allowed evicted tenants to return to their farms and re-housed others. He also promised to provide a house in Milford to shelter the poor and destitute so that they could avoid entering the workhouse. And it appears these initial gestures were no hyperbolae: in the following fourteen years, he initiated ventures to improve local business and built hotels and golf links to draw tourists. He also inaugurated a line of steamers to run between Mulroy Bay and Glasgow, via Derry, thus providing access to markets for the estate produce. On his death in 1892, he was buried near Mulroy "amid signs of mourning from the tenantry among whom he had lived and for whose benefit he had worked".

The 4th Earl's heir, Charles, was the fourth of eight children and was only thirteen years old when he inherited his father's estates and title. However, the family lived largely in London and spent little time in Ireland. After his father's death, he was sent to school at Eton and went from there to Oxford. When not at school, the new Earl joined his family in their home at 40 Portman Square. As an adult, Charles served in the South African Wars of 1899-1902 and in the First World War as a Major with the Iniskilling Fusiliers. During the War, he was known as "an epitome of aristocratic Ulster Unionism". He commanded a UVF Regiment in Donegal and arranged to run guns from Germany on board his steam yacht, the *Ganiamore.* In 1917, he became Private Secretary to the Secretary of State for the Colonies.

The heir presumptive until 1917 was Francis Patrick Clements, the third son of the 5th Earl. He joined the Navy but in May 1907, aged 22, he disappeared while staying in London and was never heard of again. In 1917, the Probate Court granted an application to presume his death.

Colonel Henry Theophilus Clements

The person who acquired Lough Rynn after Lord Leitrim's death and whose descendants inherited the estate, was Colonel Henry Theophilus Clements. He had been born at Ashfield, County Cavan and educated in England and on the Continent. He had an active public service career, holding the position of High Sheriff of Cavan in 1849 and of Leitrim in 1870; he also inherited Lord Leitrim's title of Colonel of Leitrim Militia.

The Colonel is mostly remembered for his building work on the estate. He added a new wing to the Castle, which turned the original two-storey house into a rather more imposing residence. The new extension was designed by Sir Thomas Drew, RHA and was completed in 1889. It included what became known as the 'baronial hall', with its large ornate Inglenook fireplace, heavy plaster cornices and fretted ceiling and walls wainscoted in solid English oak. Thereafter, the main hall floor of the house contained a main hall, baronial hall, chapel, reception room, living room and dining room. Two pantries, a kitchen, study, smokehouse and store were accessed by a separate entry. There were stores and a wine cellar in the basement and upstairs, fourteen bedrooms and four bathrooms.

Fig. 42: The Baronial Hall at Lough Rynn in the 20th Century (Bord Fáilte)

Colonel Clements was to manage the estate through another period of change.

By the end of the century, the tide was inexorably turning against landlordism of Lord Leitrim's type. The movement for tenants' rights had begun in earnest in the 1850s through Charles Gavan Duffy's Irish Tenant League. In 1870, Gladstone's Landlord and Tenant (Ireland) Act, although it had little actual effect, marked a turning point in the attitude of the British government to the Irish land question. From 1879, a national protest movement emerged through the Land League founded by Michael Davitt.

Lord Leitrim was assassinated in 1878, just before this time of spiralling agitation. His death—and the circumstances of it—gave the new Land League a very useful impetus and sparked a new level of outrage. From 1879, in what became known as the Land War, rural disturbances increased dramatically: a number of landlords were murdered[32] and crimes against property were prevalent, the most common being arson and the maiming of cattle. Gladstone, back in power in 1880, passed a new Land Act in 1881. Again, it was less than the agitators had wanted: this time, however, the movement stepped up the pressure. The Land League was outlawed in 1882 and replaced by The Irish National League. Under the leadership of Charles Stewart Parnell and Michael Davitt, the focus shifted from land reform and tenants' rights to Home Rule.

---

[32] On average seventeen landlords and agents were murdered each year during the Land War.

Three successive Land (Purchase) Acts in 1885, 1887 and 1891 were designed to help tenants buy land through a government-assisted scheme. The 1891 Act facilitated the creation of viable holdings in the poorest areas in the western counties from Donegal to Cork and provided a loan fund for tenants who wished to purchase their lands.

The process was completed with the Wyndham Act of 1903 which provided loans to tenants at reduced interest for the purchase of land and gave bonuses to landlords who sold. Later, the sale of land was made compulsory.

By 1921, previous tenants owned two-thirds of the land.

Lough Rynn in the 20th Century and today

Colonel Clement's son, Henry John Beresford Clements, took over the estate following his father's death in 1904. Clements lived largely at Killadoon, in Kildare, but he and his family spent about a month at Rynn each year.

According to one of his employees, Thomas Boyle, Clements was a "very good employer". In his 'Memories' of the time, Boyle recalls that there were forty-six workers on the payroll at the time, including Mr Stewart, the estate manager, Revd Joseph .G. Digges[33], chaplain, Mr Hardy the steward and a housekeeper. In addition to a weekly wage of ten shillings (about €0.63 or $0.75), all the married workers received a partly furnished house, grass for a cow or donkey, ground for sowing potatoes a good sized garden, a piece of bog for turf,

---

[33] Rev. Digges is regarded as the father of Irish beekeeping. He edited the Irish Bee Journal, later The Beekeeper's Gazette, and published 'The Irish Bee Guide': the book came to be regarded as a standard and sold 76,000 copies. Digges also helped to found the local co-operative creamery and the bank in Mohill, and was a director of the Cavan & Leitrim railway and of the Arigna mines.

and seven tons of good farm manure. Thomas describes the workers' concern over Lloyd George's Agricultural Wages Act of 1917: they were sure that Clements would dismiss a lot of the men rather than pay the newly mandated rate of 27/6 a week, a 275% increase on Boyle's previous wage. Apparently "not one man was dismissed" and Boyle is accepting of the "new contributions to be made for house rent, grazing, etc." since these deductions amounted to less than 5 shillings a week.

By 1952, when Marcus Clements inherited the estate, nearly all of the original Lough Rynn lands had been sold off by the Land Commission, mostly to descendants of the tenants of the previous century. The Clements' continued to live at Lough Rynn up to the 1970s, but on a much reduced estate.

Lough Rynn lay empty for many years after Marcus Clements and his family left Lough Rynn in the 1970s. The Castle fell into disrepair and the gardens became overgrown. In 1990, what remained of the estate was bought by Michael Flaherty, an Irish-American, and was turned for into a visitor attraction with restored gardens and pleasure walks.

In 2005, the Castle and grounds were taken over by the Hanly Group who embarked on an extensive programme of building and development, with new houses in the grounds and the Castle turned into a luxury hotel and leisure complex.

Appendix 1: Extract from *Topography of Ireland*, Samuel Lewis, 1837

Reprinted with permission from the National Library of Ireland

"MOHILL, a market and post-town, and a parish, partly in the barony and county of LONGFORD, province of LENISTER, and partly in the barony of LEITRIM, but chiefly in the barony of MOHILL, county of LEITRIM, and province of CONNAUGHT, 8½ miles (S. E.) from Carrick-on-Shannon, and 74¼ (W. N. W.) from Dublin, on the mail coach road to Sligo; containing 16,664 inhabitants, of which number, 1606 are in the town.

The town, which is neatly built, contains 305 houses; and derives its chief trade from its situation on a public thoroughfare. The market is on Thursday, and is well supplied with grain and provisions of every kind; the fairs are on the first Thursday in January, Feb. 3rd and 25th, March 17th, April 14th, May 8th, first Thursday in June, July 31st, Aug 1st and 18th, second Thursday in Sept., Oct. 19th, Nov. 10th, and the first Thursday in December. A chief constabulary force is stationed here, and petty sessions are held on alternate Saturdays.

The parish comprises 29,782 statute acres, of which 19,430 are good arable and pasture land, 60 woodland, and 10,270 are bog and waste; the soil is fertile, but the system of agriculture has hitherto been much neglected, though at present exertions are being made for its improvement. Limestone abounds and is quarried for agricultural purposes; and there are some quarries of very good freestone, which is raised for building; iron ore is found, but no mines have been yet opened. The principal seats are Clooncar, the residence of the Rev. A. Crofton; Drumard, of Theophilus B. Jones, Esq.; Drumrahan, of J. O'Brien, Esq.; Drumregan, of J. W. O'Brien, Esq.; Bonnybeg, of W. Lawder, Esq.; and Aughamore, of C. Armstrong, Esq. The scenery is greatly varied and in some parts enlivened by the river Shannon, which skirts a portion of the parish on the south west. The living is a vicarage, in the diocese of Ardagh, and in the patronage of the Bishop; the rectory is impropriate in Sir M. Crofton, Bart. The tithes amount to £651. 10. 1½ of which £218. 3. 4½ is payable to the impropriator, and the remainder to the vicar. The glebe-house was built in 1823, at an expense of £1569. 4. 7½. of which £969. 4. 7½. was a loan and £92. 6. ¾. a gift from the late Board of First Fruits; the glebe comprises 500 acres valued at £380 per annum. The church, a modern edifice, towards the erection of which the late Board of First Fruits granted a loan of £378, in 1815, is built partly on the site of the old abbey, and was recently repaired by a grant of £768 from the Ecclesiastical Commissioners. In the R. C. divisions the parish constitutes a benefice in two portions; there are chapels respectively at Mohill, Cavan, Clonturk, and Clonmorris; and there is a place of worship for Wesleyan Methodists. Nearly 700 children are taught in eight public schools, five of which are aided by an annual donation of £10 each from Lord Clements, who also gave the sites for the school houses; and there are fifteen private schools, in which are about 900 children. There are also a dispensary and a loan fund with a capital of £300. The only remains of the ancient abbey are a small circular tower; at Clonmorris are the ruins of a monastery, said to have been founded by St. Morris; and at Tullagoran is a druidical altar. There is a strong sulphureous spring at Mulock, more aperient than that of Swanlinbar; and at Athimonus, about half a mile distant, is another of similar quality."

Appendix 2: Extract from *Slater's Directory*, 1846

Reprinted with permission from the National Library of Ireland

Mohill is [ ] pleasantly situated on the sides of two gently rising hills and in a fruitful district. The town, which is the property of Sir Morgan Crofton, Bart. is composed of one main street, from which smaller ones diverge, the former consisting of several good shops, well stocked with various articles of fashion and of local requisites. The principal trade of the place is in corn, provisions, and yarn, with which it is well supplied from its populous neighbourhood. The government of the town is vested in the magistrates, who hold petty sessions once a fortnight in the sessions house. Mohill is a station for constabulary, and the revenue police, and residence of the sub-inspector of each. The public buildings are a dispensary and a fever hospital, supported in the usual way, the court house a union workhouse. There are also a loan fund and a news-room. [ ] The market, a well supplied one, is held on Thursday. There are no fewer than fifteen fairs held in the course of the year, but of these only four are chartered viz,:- February 14, April 28, July 21, and December 4. Mohill parish contained, in 1841, 17,918 inhabitants, and the town 1,626 of that number.

Post Office

Honoria Brady, Post-mistress.- Letters from all parts arrive every morning at ten minutes past seven, and are despatched every evening at a quarter before six.

Gentry & Clergy

Bohan Rev. John, c.c. Main St

Brawne Thomas, Esq. R.B. Bridge St

Clements the Hon. Lord Viscount, Loughrynn

Crofton Duke. Esq. J.P. D.P. Lakefield

Crofton Rev. Morgan, Castle St

Duke Mrs Eleanor, Bridge St.

Eivers Rev. John P.P, Main St

Hoops Rev. S.E. Hyde St

Hyde Rev. Arthur, Drumarde

Irvin Reynolds, Esq. Springfield

Jones Major T.B., Drumarde

Keirn Mr. C.M., Bridge St

Little Thomas K Esq. The Castle

O'Brien Mrs Jane, Bridge St

O'Brien John. Esq. J.P. Drumrahan

Smyth Rev. Thomas, C.C. Cavan

Vevers John Esq. (stipendiary magistrate), Castle St

Walsh Captain John H. Clooncaher

Walsh Miss -, Bridge St

Professional Persons, and School

Carleton Andrew, attorney

Duke John, Physician
Keon Terence, apothecary
Little Thos K. Land agent, The Castle
McCabe Edward, master of the national school, Main St
Nicholson John, land agent & Commissioner for affidavits Main St
O'Beirne John Physician
O'Brien Robert P. Attorney, Hyde St
Redfern Thomas, land surveyor, Treanmore
Soden Edwd. Physician & apothecary

Hotels - Posting

Kenny Henry, Main St
Little Thomas, Main St
Mulholland Ann, Main St

Public Houses

Dobson Thomas, Main St
Gannon James, Main St
O'Donnell Patrick, Main St
Reynolds Bernard, Hyde St
Ryan William, Main St

Shopkeepers and traders

Boddy James, boot & shoe maker
Brady Honoria, haberdasher
Burns Arthur, general dealer
Clarke James, baker
Cull James, dyer
Cullen Edward, process server, Castle
Donovan George, boot & shoe maker
Duignan Patrick, saddler
Fagan John, grocer & leather seller
Faughnan Hugh, general dealer
Guilday James, general dealer
Hayes Thos. Linen & woollen draper
Heany John, leather seller, Hyde St
Higgins Deuis, general dealer
Holton Phillip, general dealer
Keirnan John Linen draper
Kenny Henry, general dealer
McElroy Charles, baker
Moore Thomas, linen draper
Moxham Thos.linen & woollen draper
Murphy James, general dealer
O'Beirne John, general dealer
Reynolds Michael, linen & woollen draper
Rodaghan John, Tailor, Hyde St
Smyth William, general dealer
Soden William, grocer
Tyrrell Charles, saddler
Ward Stephen, linen & woollen draper

Places of Worship and their Ministers

PARISH CHURCH,- Rev. Arthur Hyde, rector, Drumkilla: Rev Morgan Crofton, Castle St, and Rev. S.E. Hoops, Hyde St, Curate.

RC CHAPEL- Rev. John Evers parish priest, Main St; Rev. John Bohan, Main St, and Rev. Thomas Smyth, Cavan, curates.

Public Institutions, &c.

Barrack (Constabulary), Main St
M. Keirn, sub-inspector
Barrack (Revenue Police), Thomas
Browne, Bridge St, sub-inspector;
James Coleman sub-officer
Dispensary & Fever Hospital, Main St - John Duke, M.D. Medical attendant.
Loan Fund, Main Street - Major T.B.
Jones, treasurer, Drumarde; Thos. K Little, secretary, The Castle; John
Nicholson, clerk, main St.
Sessions House, Hyde Street - William
Nicholson, clerk
Stamp Office, Main St - John
Nicholson, distributor.
Union Workhouse, Hyde St., Bartholomew Kelly, master: Jane Kelly, matron; John Clarke, clerk; John O'Beirne, M.D.

Appendix 3: Extract from *Slater's Directory*, 1881

Reprinted with permission from the National Library of Ireland

Mohill parish contained, in 1851, 11,539 inhabitants, and of the parish in 1861 was 10,303, and in 1871, 9,507, of which number the town contained 1,062.

POST OFFICE

Hyde Street, MOHILL, William McDonald, Post Master. --Letters from all parts arrive at fifteen minutes past seven morning and at thirty-five minutes past two afternoon, and are despatched at ten minutes past eleven morning and at seven evening.

Money Orders and Telegraph Office and Savings Bank.

GENTRY & CLERGY

Conefrey Rev. John, PP. Gortleteragh

Crofton Wm. Esq. Lakefield

Dobson Robert James, Esq. M.D. Fortview

Duke Mrs Eleanor, Bridge St.

Duke Mr. John, Taughlaght

Evers Very Rev. John W P.P, Main st

Hines Mr. Thomas, Wesley p

Jones Wm. Percy, Esq. J.P. The Castle

Kane John, Esq. J.P. The Castle

Kirkpatrick Mr. William, Hermitage Cottage

O'Brien Miss Alicia, -Cavan

O'Brien Robert. Esq. Gorthill

O'Shaughnesy Thomas, Esq. Hyde st

Sleven Felix, Esq. Hyde st

Thompson Folliott Wm. Esq. Main st

SCHOOLS.

NATIONAL SCHOOLS:-

Chapel lane (No. 1 boys) - John Feeny, master

Chapel lane (girls) - Taught by the Nuns

Glebe st. (No. 2) Hugh Ross, master; Kate Ross, mistress

AGENTS-MISCELLANEOUS

(See also Fire, d.c. Office Agents.)

Kane John (land), The Castle

McDonald Wm. (emigration), Hyde st

Reynold Michael (emigration), The Bridge.

ATTORNEYS.

See Solicitors.

AUCTIONEER.

Mulvany James, Hyde st

BAKERS

Burns Arthur, Main st

Cumskey Patrick, Hill st

Dooley Dennis, Hyde St

Duignan Thomas, Main St

Gray Ann, Glebe St

Harte Richard, Main St

Moore William, Glebe St

Quin J. J. & Co. Main St

Reynolds Hugh, Main St

Reynolds Michael, Main St

Reynolds Patrick, Main St

BANKS

Hibernian Bank (Branch), Hyde St- draws on Barnetts, Hoares & Co. London -- Felix Slevin, manager

Northern Banking Co. (Branch), Main st -- draws on Glyn, Mills & Co. London -- Folliott Wm Thompson. Manager.

BOOT & SHOE MAKERS.

Brady Hugh, Chapel Lane

Bridges Thomas, Main St

McCabe Francis, Glebe st

McKiernan Thomas, Chapel Hill

BUTCHERS.

Duke John, Main St

O'Donnell Henry, Main St

CARPENTERS & CART MAKERS

Shandley Wm. Castle St

Travers Patrick, Chapel Hill

Travers Thomas, Chapel Hill

PUBLIC BUILDINGS, OFFICES, &c

PLACES OF WORSHIP AND THEIR MINISTERS

PROTESTANT EPISCOPAL CHURCH,

Main st - Rev Fitzmaurice Hunt. A.M. incumbent

ROMAN CATHOLIC CHURCHES:-

Chapel Lane - Very Rev. John W. Evers P.P,; Rev. Patrick Lynch, Rev. Thomas Langan, curates. Gortleteragh - Rev. John, Confrey, PP.

METHODIST (Westleyan) CHAPEL, Main st- Ministers various

POOR LAW UNION

Workhouse, Mohill. Master - Edward Geelan; Matron - Margaret Flynn; Schoolmaster - Peter Lee; Schoolmistress - Roseanna Carney; Protestant Chaplain - Rev Fitzmaurice Hunt; Roman Catholic Chaplain- Very Rev. Canon John W. Evers. P.P.; Medical Officer - Robert J. Dobson M.D.; Clerk to the Union - Thomas Woodward. Relieving Officer - Henry Redfern, Dromodard; & James Reegan, Hyde st. Mohill.

REGISTRARS

Superintendent Registrar of Births, Deaths & Marriages - Thomas Woodward, Castle st

Registrar of Marriages - William F. Croghan, Main st

Registrar of Births, Deaths & Marriages –

Carrigallen- Michael Donoline

Mohill - Robert J. Dobson M.D.

Rowan - Calib Soden

Rynn - John Nicholls, M.D.

CHINA, GLASS, EARTHENWARE DEALERS

Duignan Thomas, Main st

Noble David, Main st

Turner Elizabeth, Main st

COOPERS

Duignan Lawrence, Glebe st

Kenny Phillip, Glebe st

FIRE & Co. OFFICE AGENTS.

English Scottish Law (life) - Wm. Kirkpatrick, Hermitage Cottage

Guardian - Thomas O'Shaughnessy, Hyde st

Royal - Wm. F. Croghan, Main st

Scottish Provincial - Felix Slevin, Hyde st

Standard (life) - W.P. Jones, J.P. Dromard

GROCERS

Burns Arthur, Main st

Chapman John, Main st

Conefrey James, Main st

Duignan Thomas, Main st

Dunne John, Main st

Elliot Frederick, Main st

Gray Ann, Glebe st

Harte Richard, Main st

Gray Ann, Glebe St

Harte Richard, Main St

McKeirnan John, Main st

Moore Wm, Glebe st

Noble David, Main st

Quin James J, Main st

Quin Wm. C, Main st

Reynolds Hugh, Main st

Reynolds Michael, Main st

Reynolds Michael, The Bridge

Reynolds Patrick, Main st

Stanley James, Main st

Whelan John, Glebe st

HARDWAREMAN

Burns Arthur, Main st

Chapman John, Main st

Duignan Thomas, Main st

Noble David, Main st

Reynolds John, Main st

Soden John, Main st

HOTELS

Burns Arthur, Main st

Hopkins John, (Commercial) Main st

Little Margaret, Main st

LINEN & WOOLLEN DRAPERS & HABERDASHERS

Burns Arthur, Main st

Croghan Wm. F, Main st

Cull James, Main st

Eginton George, Main st

Fitzpatrick John, Main st

Hayes Thomas, Main st

Stratton Robert, Main st

Ward Thomas, Main st

MILLINERS & DRESSMAKERS

Burns Arthur, Main st

Croghan Wm. F, Main st

Cull James, Main st

Eginton George, Main st

Hayes Thomas, Main st

Stratton Robert, Main st

Ward Thomas, Main st

NAIL MAKERS

Graham Thomas, Water st

Shera James, Hill st

NEWSPAPER

The Leitrim Advertiser (published every Thursday) Representatives of the late Robert Turner, Proprietors & publishers, Main st

PHYSICIANS & SURGEONS

Dobson Robert James, M.D. Fortview

Soden John (& apothecary), Main st

POSTING HOUSES.

Burns Arthur, Main st

Hopkins John, Main st

Little Margaret, Main st

SEED & GUANO DEALERS

Burns Arthur, Main st

Noble David, Main st

SOLICITORS

O'Brien Robert. Esq. Gorthill

O'Shaughnest Thomas, Hyde st

SPIRIT & PORTER RETAILERS

Bierne Michael, Hyde st

Burns Arthur, Main st

Conefrey James, Main st

Duignan Thomas, Main st

Dunne John, Main st

Fanning Catherine, Glebe st

Farrelly John, Main st

Gray Ann, Glebe St

Harte Richard, Main St

Gray Ann, Glebe St

Harte Richard, Main St

McKenna John, Hyde st

McKeirnan John, Main st

Noble David, Main st

Quin James J, Main st

Quin Wm. C, Main st

Reynolds Hugh, Main st

Reynolds Michael, Main st

Reynolds Michael, The Bridge

Reynolds Patrick, Main st

Soden John, Main st

Stanley James, Main st

Whelan John, Glebe st

TAILORS

Gray Michael, Main st

Ryan Bernard, Hyde st

TIMBER & IRON MERCHANTS

Burns Arthur, Main st

Farrell John, Main st

Noble David, Main st

Reynolds John, Main st

WOOLLEN DEALERS

See Linen & Woollen Drapers

Miscellaneous

Dobson William, leather seller, Main st

Johnstone Jeremiah, blacksmith, Hyde street.

Mc Guinness James, barony cess collector, Hyde st.

Mulvany James, broker &c. Hyde st

Nicholson John, Commissioner for taking affidavits & master extraordinary in chancery, Main st

Soden John (& apothecary), Main st

Turner Elizabeth, printer & stationer, & tea dealer, Main st.

Barrack (Constabulary), Glebe street - John McGovern, sub-inspector; Thomas Wheelan, head constable

Convent, Chapel lane - Sister Mary; Josephine, superiores

Dispensary, Main st - Robert J. Dobson M.D. Medical attendant

Sessions House, Hill st - William Nicholson, clerk

Stamp Office, Main st - Bernard G. Cull, sub-distributor

CAR

To DROMOD, Mail Car, from the Post Office, every morning at ten minutes past eleven.

CONVEYANCE BY RAILWAY

The nearest station in Dromod, on the Midland Great Western Line, five miles distant. For conveyance thereto, see car

Appendix 4: List of tenants on Lough Rynn Estate

Reprinted with permission from the National Library of Ireland

Tenant	Townland	Acres, Roods, Perches	Rent	Lease Agreement date	Signed on
Robert Bell Coote	Tryne (Trean)	78 2 24	£52.0. 0	29 Sep 1865	12 Mar 1866
James Bohan	Tulcon	9 2 35	£7.4.0	29 Sep 1863	6 Feb 1864
James Bohan	Tulcon	9 2 22	£7.4.0	29 Sep 1866	5 Nov 1867
Mathew Conefrey	Farnaught	1 0 39	£2.0.0	23 Aug1862	29 Sep 1854
Thomas Connell	Tooman	2 1 24	£2.12.0	2 Sep 1874	2 Jan 1875
Widow May Connell	Tooman	2 2 5	£2.12. 0	29 Sep 1874	2 Jan 1875
Mary Connell	Tooman	2 3 30	£2.18.0	29 Sep 1876	22 Mar 1877
Thomas Connor	Tulcon (Clooncahir)	14 1 9	£10.16.0	29 Sep 1865	5 Feb 1866
Jane Cox	Tooman	3 0 39	£3.0.0	29 Sep 1876	17 Mar 1877
Patrick Cox No. 2	Tooman	9 1 18	£7.0.0	29 Sep 1874	1 Jan 1875
James Creegan	Farnaught	2 1 28	£3.0.0	22 Aug 1862	29 Sep 1854
John Crowe	Gortletteragh	39 1 38½	£30.6.0	30 Mar 1865	29 Sep 1864
Susannah Crowe	Tryne (Trean)	63 0 3	£50.0.0	29 Sep 1865	3 Mar 1866
Michael Duignan	Gortletteragh	12 3 4	£8.0.0	22 Aug 1862	29 Sep 1854
Francis Flynn	Gortletteragh	5 0 20	£4.0.0	2 Apr 1879	29 Sep 1878
Edward Geelan	Tooman	0 3 34	£1.10.0	29 Sep 1875	28 Feb 1876
Lawrence Kelleher	Tooman	3 1 15	£2.12.0	29 Sep 1875	3 Mar 1876
Thomas Kelly	Gortletteragh	20 1 7	£15.0.0	10 Feb 1864	29 Sep 1863
Thomas Kelly	Gortletteragh	20 1 7	£16.5.0	31 Mar 1870	29 Sep 1868
Denis Mahon	Tooman	4 0 0	£3.16.0	29 Sep 1876	22 Mar 1877
Catherine McDonagh	Tooman	0 3 6	£1.0. 0	29 Sep 1876	17 Mar 1877
Thomas Reynolds	Farnaught	10 1 26	£3.0.0	25 Aug 1862	29 Sep 1854
Thomas Reynolds	Gortletteragh	11 3 31	£8.0.0	25 Aug 1862	29 Sep 1854

Tenant	Townland	Acres, Roods, Perches	Rent	Lease Agreement date	Signed on
Antony Reynolds	Tryne (Trean)	21 3 18	£16.17.6	29 Sep 1861	27 June 1862
John Reynolds	Tryne (Trean)	38 0 10	£24.0.0	29 Sep 1854	19 Aug 1862
Michael Rogan	Gortletteragh	16 3 5	£12.0.0	15 Aug 1862	29 Sep 1858

Bibliography

The manuscript material, contemporary accounts, newspapers and books listed below do not represent a complete bibliography but comprise the main sources for references and facts used throughout this book.

Annual Reports of the Poor Law Commissioners, 1838-50

Brownrigg, Sir Henry John, Report on the State of Ireland 1863; NLI Ms 915

Census of Ireland, 1841, 1851, 1861

Cholera Papers 1832

Devon Commission Report, 1844, 1845

Griffiths Valuations, Union of Mohill, 1857

Journal of Lady Caroline Clements to Paris and Return to England 1815

Larcom Papers, 1856–1863

(Letters, memoranda and news cuttings concerning the state of Co. Leitrim with special reference to crime); Ms 7634

Larcom Papers, 1868 (State of Ireland; agrarian outrages); NLI Ms 7613

Last Will and Testament of Nathaniel Clements 1854

Leitrim Papers: Observations by Clements on the state of tenant holdings, 1838–'39; Ms 12,788

Leitrim Papers: Notebooks re Lord Leitrim's estate 1800-1829; Mss 12,790 – 12,804; Sydney Clements, Letters, MS 33,849

Leitrim Estate Papers Mohill/Lough Rynn Estate 1749 – 1895: Leases and Agreements; Ms 33,816;

Lord Leitrim on Agrarian Crime, 1846–1861; NLI Ms 21,753

Mohill Board of Guardians 1845-1859

National Archives of Ireland

Outrage Papers for County Leitrim 1850-1852 and 1799-1852, Public Records Office Dublin

Papers relating to the Relief and Distress and the State of the Unions in Ireland.

Personal Accounts of the 3rd Earl of Leitrim, 1832–1848

Poor Law Records

Recipe Books from Lough Rynn

Relief Commission Papers

Rentals for Lord Leitrim's Estate, 1837–1842 ; Mss 12,787

Rent Roll, March 25 1801; Ms 12,789

Rentals for Lord Leitrim's Estate, 1838–41; c.1853; c.1859; c.1860; c.1868;Mss 5,728 – 5,733

Rentals for Lord Leitrim's Estate, 1842, 1843; Ms 12,809

Rentals for Lord Leitrim's Estate, 1842-1855; Mss 5,803 – 5,805

Rentals for Lord Leitrim's Estate, 1844-'45, 1845-'46, 1847-'48;Mss 12,810 – 12,812

Rentals for Lord Leitrim's Estate, 1853, 1856-'57, 1862, 1864-'69; Mss 3,803 – 3,812

Rent Ledgers for Lord Leitrim's Estate 1855-'69; Mss 5,794 – 5,802

Weekly Labour Returns for Lord Leitrim's Estate 1838–1860; Mss 3026–3029

Sir Robert Peel Papers 1842–1846 ; British Library Mss 35,799 f.261; 40613 f.105b; 40586 ff.115, 117; 40442 ff.98-104; 40509 f.338; 40592 f.292

Earl of Harwicke Papers; Ms 35,799 f.261

Lord Wellesley Papers 1834; Ms 37,306 f.400

Historical Journals of Ardagh & Clonmacnoise Antiquarian Society, 1945

Macvey Napier Papers Vol VII 1835; Ms 34617 f. 515

Letter Book of Lord Worthington in Ireland 1783-1784 Ms 38716 f. 37, 38

Irish Press 2/10/1967 (Brady, Séamus, Secret Diaries of the 3rd Earl) Ballinamore

Punch, 24 October 1863

Slater's Directory Ballinamore File 32

Statistical & Social Inquiry Society of Ireland Journal, Vol .IV, 1864

The Leitrim & Longford Advertiser, Mohill 1867–1878

The Leitrim Journal & Carrick-on-Shannon Advertiser, 1850–1853

The Annals of Clonmacnoise

The Annals of Loch Cé

The Annals of the Four Masters

Bence-Jones, Mark, *Burke's Guide to Country Houses, Vol.11, Ireland,* 1978

Burke, Sir Bernard and Burke, Ashworth P *A Genealogical & Heraldic History of the Peerage and Baronetage,* London 1915

Clement, Percival Wood, *Ancestors and Descendants of Robert Clements Vol I & II,* Philadelphia 1937

Dolan, Liam, *The Third Earl of Leitrim*, 1978

Doubleday, HA and de Walden, Lord Howard, Editors *The Complete Peerage* Vol VII *by G.E.C.*, London 1929

Foster, RF *Modern Ireland 1600–1972*, Penguin, 1989

Guckian, Des, *Leitrim and Longford 1798 "Undaunted by Gibbet and Yeos"*

Hoppen, K Theodore, *Elections, Politics & Society in Ireland 1832–1885*, 1984

Kelly, Fr. Liam, *A Flame Now Quenched Rebels and Frenchmen in Leitrim*

Kerr, Donal *The Catholic Church and the Famine*, Dublin: Columbia Press, 1996

Kineally, Christine This Great Calamity: The Irish Famine 1845-52, 2006

Lewis, Samuel *Topographical Dictionary of Ireland, 1837*

Litton, Helen, *The Irish Famine: An Illustrated History, Wolfhound Press, 1994*

Lodge, Edmund *The Peerage and Baronetage of the British Empire*, London 1888

MacAtasney, Gerard *Leitrim and the Great Hunger*, Carrick-on-Shannon & District Historical Society, 1997

Moody TW, Martin FX, Byrne FJ (Edit), *A New History of Ireland: III. Early Modern Ireland 1534-1691,* Clarendon Press Oxford 1976

Moody TW, Martin FX, Byrne FJ (Edit), *A New History of Ireland: IX. Maps, Genealogies, Lists,* Clarendon Press Oxford 1984

Moody TW, Vaughan WE (Edit), *A New History of Ireland: III. Eighteenth Century Ireland 1691-1800,* Clarendon Press Oxford 1986

Moran, Laurence *History of the Crofton Estate*

O'Shaughnessy, Mark S, *On Criminal Statistics Especially with Reference to Population, Education and Distress in Ireland*

Pakenham, Thomas, *The Year of Liberty The Great Irish Rebellion of 1798*

The Fanad Patriots: Full authentic story of the killing of Lord Leitrim April 1878 Letterkenny, 1962

Sexton, Regina in *The Encyclopaedia of Ireland*, ed. Brian Lalor, Gill & Macmillan, 2003

Thomson, David, *Woodbrook*, Vintage London, 1991

Vaughan WE (Edit), *A New History of Ireland: V. Ireland Under the Union Vol I 1801-1870,* Clarendon Press Oxford 1989

Vaughan WE (Edit), *A New History of Ireland: V. Ireland Under the Union Vol II 1870-1921,* Clarendon Press Oxford 1996

Whelan, Michael, *The Parish of Aughavas, Co. Leitrim,* Michael Whelan, 1998

www.mohill.com

www.fenagh.com

www.castlebar.ie

www.quinnipiac.edu

Index